W9-BRO-313

Teaching *Safe* Horsemanship

A Guide to English & Western Instruction

Jan Dawson

A Storey Publishing Book

STOREY

Storey Communications, Inc.

*The mission of Storey Communications is to serve our customers
by publishing practical information that encourages personal independence
in harmony with the environment.*

Edited by Diana Delmar
Design and production by Meredith Maker
Production assistance by Erin Lincourt
Cover photograph by Kevin Kennefick
Line drawings by Elayne Sears. Pages 23 and 30, line drawings by LaNelle
Indexed by Susan Olason, Indexes & Knowledge Maps

Special thanks to Carolyn Henderson for the use of Clover Hill Farm, Williamstown, MA, where we photographed the front cover. Thanks also to Lynne Cox, Michele Barnard, Debbie Bullett, and "Cassie".

Copyright © 1997 by Jan Dawson

All rights reserved. No part of this book may be reproduced without written permission from the publisher, except by a reviewer who may quote brief passages or reproduce illustrations in a review with appropriate credits; nor may any part of this book be reproduced, stored in a retrieval system, or transmitted in any form or by any means — electronic, mechanical, photocopying, recording, or other —without written permission from the publisher.

The information in this book is true and complete to the best of our knowledge. All recommendations are made without guarantee on the part of the author or Storey Communications, Inc. The author and publisher disclaim any liability in connection with the use of this information. For additional information, please contact Storey Communications, Inc., Schoolhouse Road, Pownal, Vermont 05261.

The legal information contained in this book is for general information only. It is not intended to be, nor should it be understood to replace, legal advice. Rendering legal advice requires an attorney-client relationship, and the relationship between the author/publisher is in no way intended as a substitute for the attorney-client relationship.

Every effort has been made to make the legal information in this book current, comprehensive, and accurate, but laws are different from state to state and change over time; therefore, no warranty is given as to the legal information provided.

The reader is urged to consult an attorney in his or her own state for specific legal advice.

Storey Publishing books are available for special premium and promotional uses and for customized editions. For further information, please call the Custom Publishing Department at 1-800-793-9396.

Printed in Canada by Transcontinental Printing
10 9 8 7 6 5 4 3 2 1

Library of Congress Cataloging-in-Publication Data

Dawson, Jan, 1943-
    Teaching safe horsemanship : a guide to English & Western instruction
        p. cm.
    "A Storey Publishing Book"
    Includes bibliographical references and index.
    ISBN 0-88266-972-9 (hc : alk. paper)
    1. Horsemanship—Study and teaching.   2. Western riding—Study and teaching.   I. Title.
SF310.5.D38   1997
798.2'3'071—dc21
                                                97-648
                                              CIP

CONTENTS

DEDICATION

To my husband, Bob, who gave me the fanciest pickup west of the Mississippi and an imported German horse to haul around. And to Bruce Blake of Lexington Safety Products, whose grant made the research for this book possible.

ACKNOWLEDGMENTS

This handbook was four years in production, including two years of testing in the field. All this was preceded by 10 years of research. Consequently, I have an incredibly long list of people to acknowledge.

Without the tolerance and support of my husband, Bob, this handbook never would have come into being, even in draft form. Bob patiently edited the first draft, wrote the legal articles, and did — and still does — all of the legal research.

My patient colleagues, now vice presidents of AAHS, kindly field-tested the handbook. They are Jane Kellerman, Nancy Lanzer, and Brenda Tallmon. Their help was invaluable. The four of us used the first year's experiences at many instructor certification clinics to produce the standardized curriculum that our clinicians now use.

Without riding students we would have gone nowhere, and we thank all those students who have been unwitting participants in the development of this handbook and the related program.

All the instructor candidates made significant contributions. Without them we would not know for sure whether this system worked. We teach instructors, who then teach students, who tell us one way or another whether they have been taught successfully.

The students pictured in this book — some beginners, some not — were generous with their time and exhibited great patience. They are Emily Burden, Barbie Friesenhahn, Royal Fritsch, Jeff Pendleton, Carina Pinales, Jennifer Raske, and Keri Kaye Ward. They were supported by Brandy, Casanova, Mac, and Soni, all school horses; Victorian Angel, Barbie's horse; and Magic Cascaron, the photographer's horse.

And most importantly, I would like to thank Carole Chiles Fuller, the editor of the original version of this handbook and the photographer for most of the photos in this volume. She kept me sane, and her professional judgment and expertise were critical to the book's completion. Carole is herself an accomplished dressage rider, which made the job easier for both of us.

Many thanks also to Richard Raske and Dick Pond, who also took photographs for this book.

The following people have been the inspiration for this instructor-training system and the book. Their influence has been tremendous, and it has been an honor to know and work with them. They are Ray Hunt, Col. K. Albrecht von Ziegner, Paul Kathen, Ann Rickard, Jackie Krshka, Ed Wintz, Tommy Cullen, Don Offerman — who dared me to show a reiner, taught me how, and even loaned me his great horse, and Susan and Wayne Pooley — who taught me about the real world of competitive Western riding.

Special thanks to Lexington Safety Products Inc., whose grant made this project possible. Thank you all.

— Jan Dawson
September 1996

A FOUNDATION FOR TEACHING SAFE HORSEMANSHIP

For quite some time before this handbook was even an idea, I had become uncomfortable with the approach to horsemanship safety as it was often practiced and with the meaning of phrases such as "correct riding" and "quality riding instruction."

Obvious safety measures weren't consistently employed by stables with beginners in their student ranks. Some instructors seemed to put even less emphasis on basic safety measures for riders with more advanced skills. I encountered teachers who wouldn't take the very risks they were asking me to take, even though they were considered top-notch instructors. I often ended up training someone else's misbehaving horse.

It seemed to me that for riding to be correct, it should be safe — that safe riding *is* correct riding — and that this philosophy should be the foundation for quality riding instruction. Hence, the development of this handbook.

This is not a book that teaches how to train horses. Nor is it a book that teaches riding. *This is a book that teaches one person how to teach another person how to ride. It's about how to have an effective and safe teaching program.*

A. What Is Quality Riding Instruction?

To provide quality instruction, three themes must prevail:
1. First is physical safety: Helmets must be worn, the facility and surrounds must be safe for riding, and the stable must be managed in such a way that it remains safe for students.

Correct riding is safe riding is correct riding is safe riding . . .

2. Second is a positive instructor attitude toward the student. Is the instructor really looking after the student? Does the student's horse have a problem? Is the student capable of doing what she's being asked to do, and is the risk she's being asked to take reasonable? Can she foresee the risks that might be involved?

3. Third is instructor competency. The instructor should be able to explain and demonstrate the skills in such a way that the student can learn them.

Horses don't have training wheels — nor can an instructor balance and control the horse by holding the reins and the back of the saddle, as a parent might hold the handlebars and backseat of a bicycle. Therefore, teaching beginners to ride horses presents some difficult and serious safety issues. The riding instructor usually cannot step in and take over at will.

The serious safety issues that apply to beginning riders, however, cannot be separated from the riding skills that are taught to students at any level. Lessons must be kept at a manageable pace — well within the skill level of the rider. Ultimately, it is learned skill and judgment that will keep a rider and horse safe.

Throughout my riding career, I have questioned the prevailing attitude about riding lessons in general. Many books try to show the less-gifted, novice rider just what it is that the talented or natural rider "feels" in hopes that this feeling can be taught. These books often usually leave out an important fact: it is often the less gifted but more dedicated student who ultimately excels because he has had to work hard all along. Other books go to the other extreme and acknowledge no feeling at all with riding.

If we attempted to teach bicycle riding in the same way that the vast majority of students are taught to ride, most people would give up because of so many falls. Most riding instruction involves one person — the instructor — telling another person — the student — where to put her body parts in space. For example: head up, heels down, sit up, turn your shoulders. The result is often a stiff rider.

Why? Students are being taught to pose on a horse, then ride while posed. It is difficult to concentrate on both posing and riding. Posing presupposes stiffness, and stiffness causes falls. Rarely will anyone learn to ride by learning to pose — unless she is a natural. Riders learn to ride by being taught exercises that enable them to feel. **First one moves with the horse, then one directs the horse by interfering with his movement. *This* is riding from your seat.**

In addition, what many instructors say is not what they mean — or they say what they mean but it's not what the student hears. Let's take the old standby, "Put your heels down." Most beginners interpret this as "Jam your lower leg forward so your heels seem down."

Because we all know that the dedicated rider of average talent often will achieve more than the gifted rider who is less dedicated, we base this book on the premise that the same is true of instructors. A dedicated instructor of average talent can learn to be an excellent instructor through thoughtful study and practice.

A note on gender issues: His and her are used interchangeably in this book. No gender bias is intended.

Throughout the book, you'll notice repetition. This is intentional. I've found that repetition is the surest way to grill home a point, particularly if I cannot ask each student to summarize after every chapter.

Safety, of course, is emphasized and especially the use of safety equipment, particularly helmets. Other safety equipment, such as sturdy boots with a heel, also are important, but helmets lead the list of important safety gear. A foot injury while riding is unlikely to be fatal, but a head injury could be. So wear a helmet. Wear a helmet every time you ride or handle a horse.

Lexington Safety Products

Only professional crash dummies or dummy wanna-bes ride without helmets. Helmets are important — wear one.

The first version of this handbook, in fact, was produced with a grant from Lexington Safety Products Inc., which makes helmets. We assume that only professional crash dummies or dummy wanna-bes ride without helmets. *If you permit riding without helmets at your facility or in your lessons or on a trail ride that you are guiding, and there is an accident resulting in a head injury, some lawyer will winter in the Bahamas at your expense.*

Most accidents happen because people fall off horses due to somebody's bad judgment. This handbook is aimed at preventing accidents that arise from bad judgment on the horse and on the ground. Bad judgment means you should have anticipated and prevented the accident, but didn't; if you're unlucky, it also will mean you'll get sued.

In order to reduce the time of extreme vulnerability for beginning riding students of all ages, I have tried to articulate the system we use to teach people to sit securely and safely on horses as quickly as possible. I state safety rules, but the emphasis of this handbook is to encourage novice and experienced instructors to think, to think ahead, and to plan. Horsemanship safety is a philosophy.

Most accidents are foreseeable and, thus, avoidable. This means that to allow them to happen is carelessness; carelessness is negligence. Learn to think ahead, protect your students, and yourself. Protect your students.

B. Litigation Resistance and Safety Concerns

This is the handbook used for riding instructors who are certified or are seeking certification by the American Association for Horsemanship Safety Inc. (AAHS). It also is intended for use by those seeking other AAHS certifications, such as the non-riding supervisors of schools, barns, and horse shows, as well as assistant riding instructors, and for riding instructors who simply wish to improve their lesson programs without the immediate goal of certification.

Certification, however, is important. Why? It documents credentials. The consumer can find out something about the instructor's training. But why is it important from a safety point of view? Easy. To prevent the less experienced instructors from learning the hard way — at their students' expense — and to solidify for the experienced instructors the principles they use unconsciously so that they become a real part of the lesson.

Why AAHS certification? Safety is safety, right? Not necessarily. Safety is a philosophy. Correct riding is safe riding at every level of skill or risk. We all say we are interested in safety, and certainly no one wants to see students hurt. But the desire to be safe may not be a sufficient motivator to get an instructor or supervisor, novice or old hand to rethink or even think through every lesson and every situation — habitually. On the other hand the threat of a lawsuit and the realization that no one is really judgment-proof is a great motivator.

Understanding the origin of a lawsuit and what kind of accidents generate lawsuits can turn a careless, lazy instructor into a thinking, planning instructor — or a retired instructor. It's your choice.

Let's face it: We've always had the opportunity to implement safety measures that would prevent injuries. But it wasn't until lawsuits came along and our liability insurance rates soared that many instructors began to pay real attention to safety issues, and then it was because they *had* to.

A major goal of the AAHS safety program, therefore, is to show AAHS instructors, their employers, and their employees how to insulate themselves from lawsuits resulting from negligence in horse-related accidents. AAHS's primary objective is to promote safety on and around horses by training better instructors and riders. AAHS–certified instructors first and foremost are lifeguards. Their training focuses on providing a safe riding environment. The safe riding environment includes activities around the horse and on the horse, activities involving the horse during routine training, boarding, showing, lessons, and pleasure riding.

It is not AAHS's intention to favor one style of riding over another. However, the association is concerned with correct balance on any type of horse and with an AAHS instructor's ability to assist students in finding their balances as safely and quickly as possible.

As a riding instructor, your philosophy must be the philosophy promoted by John Lyons:

Human safety is first.
Horse safety is second.
Everything else is third.

It is not within the parameters of this book to teach an instructor candidate how to ride. The AAHS expects candidates to be competent riders. They should be able to demonstrate and explain the aids for the following skills when they present for certification:
- Walk
- Trot or jog
- Canter or lope in both directions on the correct lead
- Halt

- Rein back
- Counter canter
- Leg yield or side pass
- Figure 8 at a trot
- Figure 8 at a lope or canter with change of lead through the trot

This handbook should enable the instructor to do the following:
- Explain how a lawsuit comes about and how to avoid one. (Remember, lawsuits have been a greater motivator for safety than has safety for safety's sake.)
- Improve teaching skills.
- Set a riding standard that each instructor must meet.
- Heighten awareness of safety issues and their importance.
- Supply basic plans and guidelines for the more common horse activities.
- Teach emergency strategy thinking.

This handbook is intended as a reference and guide. A recommended reading list appears on page 147.

C. The Rules

Experienced, competent riding instructors or trainers will do many things automatically, sometimes unconsciously. They will have developed a safe routine the hard way — by making the mistakes or by having accidents. Only a few will have had the formal training similar to that formerly found in cavalry schools or with cavalry-trained instructors. These instructors or trainers will automatically evaluate horses and riders. But this comes only with experience.

Although they may be competent riders, unseasoned instructors often won't have the experience to make the judgment calls. In our AAHS clinics, we prefer to teach just a few principles, but they encompass many rules. However, we recognize that many people still want the short, quick answer. Maybe it's the MTV approach to teaching ground safety. For those people, some of the rules follow. You may develop more.

If what you plan to do is prohibited by any rule on this list and you do it anyway, and if there is an accident that would have been prevented by following this rule, you may expect a letter from the injured person's attorney. There is no such thing as a complete list — so don't think this is all there is — and there may be situations in which a given rule may not apply.

Many of these rules are presented as if to a student; **however, what we teach must be what we do, or we still can get in trouble. The words we never want to hear from one of our students or customers on the witness stand after an accident are, "I know that's what she always told us to do, but what she always did was . . . so we did it the way she did." This is no way to try to convince someone you are truly committed to safety.**

Follow the Hard Line, Bold Face, Black Letter Safety Rules for:

- Approaching
- Handling
- Leading and Turnout
- Tying
- Bridling
- Saddling

- Mounting and Dismounting
- Arena Etiquette
- Trail Riding
- Trailering
- Facility
- Fences and Gates

Rules for Approaching

1. Wear your ASTM/SEI–approved protective helmet whenever you are working around horses or riding them. Sturdy boots with a heel are a good idea and so are protective vests for some types of riding, but a helmet is the most important piece of safety equipment there is for riding.
2. Let the horse know you are coming. Speak or whistle. Watch for an ear or a look to acknowledge your presence and tell you it's OK.
3. Approach the shoulder from an angle. The horse's vision is impaired directly in front and in back. That's where predators go, because the horse can't see them.
4. Walk and speak normally. Do not run or creep. Do not shout or whisper.

Rules for Handling

1. While working around horses, stay close so you won't get the full impact of a kick, or walk 12 feet or more from the nearest part of the horse, which should be out of kicking range. Fifteen feet is even better. There is no safe place to be without paying close attention to the horse within 12 to 15 feet all the way around him. Let your arm pass behind the horse first before your body passes behind him, keeping your arm where it protects your rib cage but touches the horse the entire time — not on top of the horse's rump.
2. An instructor should ride all lesson or trail horses and get to know each and their individual temperaments before exposing students to them.
3. Let the horse know what you intend to do before you do it. For example, don't just grab a foot; run your hand down the leg and ask the horse to lift his foot. If he knows you are going to lift a foot, he also knows you are not going to do anything else — like maybe attack or eat him.
4. Tying or holding the head provides the most safety when working around a horse.
5. Always keep a hand on the horse and talk to him so he doesn't forget where you are — or go to sleep only to be surprised by your touch later.
6. Always tie with a quick-release knot that can be pulled loose even after the horse sits back. A daisy chain works best.
7. Keep a knife or hatchet handy so you can cut a horse loose quickly if he's tied incorrectly and an emergency arises.

8. Try to do what you have to do around a horse as close to the shoulder as possible. He can still kick you, but it's more difficult.

9. Never stand directly in front of a horse, because he can't see you well. When the horse can't see you, he may feel threatened.

10. Never stand directly behind a horse, even when braiding, washing, or thinning his tail, because he can't see you. Always stand off to one side, facing his rump. Bring the tail to you and keep an eye on his ears, or have someone watch the ears for you. If someone can hold the head, it is even better.

11. Never reach for a horse's head or nose. You could scare the horse by having your hand suddenly enter his field of vision. If you must pet or brush his face, start at the shoulder and work forward. In the wild, one wolf goes for the nose while the rest of the pack goes for the kill.

12. Never walk under or step over the tie rope. The horse may choose that moment to stomp a fly or spook forward. A person may get a knee in the mouth or be squashed against the wall or post.

13. When applying hoof oil or wrapping bandages, squat, don't kneel. You can spring away faster.

14. When cleaning his feet, keep your own feet out of the area where the horse will put his. He may put his there sooner than you think.

15. **Do not hand feed your horses!** Feed treats in their feeder or in a bucket you may hold. They will still know who gave them the treats and are less likely to go searching for carrots among fingers.

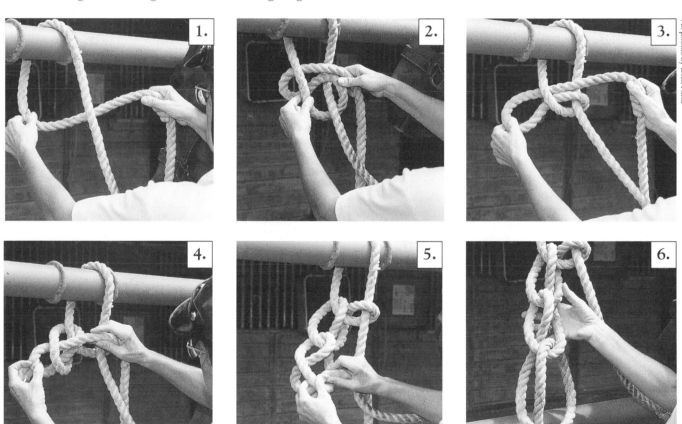

All photos by Dick Pond

Use a quick-release knot that you can untie speedily even if the horse sits back. A daisy chain works best. Follow the steps shown to make a daisy chain.

When picking out hooves, keep your own feet out of the area where the horse will put his foot down.

Treats can be fed from a bucket. Horses will still appreciate receiving them — and you'll keep all your fingers intact.

16. Stay with a tied horse. If you can't stay with him, don't tie him.

17. Work quietly, with no sudden movements or noises.

18. Be calm and confident; a nervous or timid handler causes a wary, or suspicious, unsafe horse.

19. Keep your balance and don't drop your grooming tools. Klutzes often get stepped on.

20. Know not only each horse's temperament, but also the peculiarities of each horse. An instructor should take those into consideration and share this information with an appropriate rider.

21. Never tease a horse. He could develop dangerous habits. Dangerous horses seldom lead long, happy lives. Keep your sense of humor if a horse teases you.

22. If the horse misbehaves, never punish in anger. Try redirecting his attention. Know the difference between discipline and revenge.

23. If you must discipline a horse, do it instantly. You only have a few seconds or he will not be able to connect the punishment with the bad behavior. Never strike the horse on or near his head or, better, never in front of the shoulder.

24. Turned-out horses should not wear halters. Halters can catch on posts and feet, and some halters shrink. If it is absolutely necessary for a turned-out horse to wear a halter, use a breakable leather halter or one of the nylon halters with a breakaway leather crown. Check the horse daily.

25. Wear boots or hard-toed shoes that tie whenever you work around a horse. If boots make riding safer, they make handling horses safer, too. No tennis shoes, sandals, or loafers, please. Some brands of riding shoes are okay, too, but if they have rubber soles, don't put them in stirrups with rubber pads because they'll stick, just like rubber boots will.

26. Never leave students without supervision. Advanced students need supervision; all children and novices — even adult novices — should have constant supervision.

27. Discourage the handling of horses when someone is completely alone, especially your customers. Do not permit riding unless a staff member is on the premises and is aware of the rider.

28. Be careful with cross ties, especially with a horse that's not used to them. If you use cross ties, have an escape route on three sides in case the horse panics.

Guidelines for Using Cross Ties

- They should attach only slightly higher than the horse's head.
- Panic snaps should connect the tie to the halter.
- The rope should be breakable or elastic.
- The rope should attach comfortably but not be overly loose. The horse should be able to move its head about six inches left and right.
- There should always be a partition behind the horse so he is not invited to pull back.
- There should be a rubber mat, dirt floor, or other nonslick surface under his feet.
- The ties should not be overly long — maximum of 12 to 15 feet for both ropes together.
- Know that cross ties can be extremely dangerous for both horse and human.

Rules for Leading and Turnout

1. Hold the lead rope with your right hand immediately below, not on, the snap. A knot in the tail end helps prevent the end of the lead from slipping through your fingers.
2. Fold the rest of the rope in your left hand. Don't let it drag.
3. Never hold loops or put your arm through loops. This also applies to longe lines.
4. When haltering or unhaltering, let the lead drop to the ground, or, better, place it over the horse's neck and hold it for better control. If you lay the lead over your arm and the horse jerks away, you may catch a loop. You can always catch the horse later.
5. The horse should walk beside you, not in front or behind. The safest place for the handler is at the horse's side, between his head and shoulder. Nowhere is safe for children too little to control the horse's head. Remember, nowhere around the horse is totally safe. Horses can bite or spook. They can kick at a fly and inadvertently kick you. Be vigilant.
6. When turning the horse, try to turn to the right and walk around him. This is difficult for small people to do without stepping in the way of the horse's front feet, unless the horse is extremely well trained. If you must turn the horse to the left, step back so that the horse passes in front of you. *Stay out from in front of his front feet.* If he spooks, he needs room to go by you, not over you.
7. Hold your elbow out if you need to push the horse away if he gets too close or acts up.
8. Children should not lead big horses without constant supervision.
9. Although you should always try to lead from the left, instructors should train their horses to handle from both sides in case a student makes a mistake. (Same for mounting.)
10. A horse is big and strong. If he insists on leading, don't try to get in front of him to stop him. You won't succeed unless he decides to let you. Such a horse needs to be trained to lead properly by an experienced horse handler.
11. If the horse attempts to pull away, don't hang on and get dragged. Catch him later.

12. Don't put the lead rope around any part of your body or tie it to you. No joke, it's been done!

13. When tying the horse, keep your fingers out of the loops and knots. Keep your fingers out of reins, bridle parts, and girth buckles. Students must consciously protect themselves in ways experienced instructors, trainers, and riders do by habit. Protect your fingers; they won't grow back.

14. At gates and doors, the horse should stop and wait so that the handler can step through. The handler then steps aside to allow the horse to pass through. Stall doors and gates are not big enough for both of you. A horse in the habit of going first will trample a handler who stumbles. Worse yet, when the horse goes ahead, his hind feet pass the handler too closely.

15. Lead horses with proper lead ropes, not lariats, longe lines, or anything else that is excessively long or not designed for that purpose. You could get tangled up and so could the horse.

16. When getting a horse out of his stall, wait to enter the stall until he turns and faces the door. Don't go into the stall if the horse won't turn and face you, or if he has his ears back.

17. When turning the horse loose in the stall or in the pasture, lead him all the way through the door or gate, close the gate, turn him around to face the door or gate, then let him go. You don't want to walk back by his hind end to get out and you don't want his flying heels to pass your head as he gallops off — they might not pass your (let us hope) helmeted head.

18. Don't allow students to get horses out or put horses back without supervision.

19. Train horses to be let loose quietly. If the horse wants to jerk away, he should be retrained by a staff person. Take a little feed in a bucket to give him a treat after you let him go, not before, so he will stop thinking about jerking away and running off. Don't do this each time, just often enough to keep his

Post safety rules on large signs. The signs can be designed to appeal to children.

hopes up. Use extra care if he is turned out with other horses. Turn him loose first, if possible, so he won't have other horses to run toward. Eventually, with consistent handling, he will forget about breaking away.

20. Stall doors should be all the way open or all the way shut. A partially open door invites a horse to attempt an exit during which he could crush a shoulder or a hip — his or the handler's. Swinging doors are a hazard, but if you have them, they should swing outward, not into the stall.

21. It is a bad idea to attempt to clean a stall with a horse in it. If it must be done, tie him. Horses can and have jumped wheelbarrows. It also is easy to poke the horse accidentally with the manure fork. Remember, if the horse is tied, he should not be left unattended.

Rules for Tying

1. A good rule is "eye high and arm's length" — that is, the horse's eye and the handler's arm. Tied too low, the horse can get tangled in the rope or sit back and damage his spine. Too long a rope also can cause a tangle, and if he sits back, he'll suffer a bigger jolt when he hits the end of the rope. He also will be able to reach around and bite the person working near him, or be able to get a leg over the rope.

2. Always tie with a quick-release knot. A daisy chain to the end of the rope works well. That takes care of the tail of the lead, and it won't tighten so hard that you can't get it loose if the horse sits back. (See Handling, Rule 6.)

3. Keep a big knife or a hatchet handy for the stuck, bound, or knotted rope in an emergency.

4. Never tie with bridle reins. The horse can break the reins, injure his mouth, or even break his jaw.

5. Tie to something solid. Use a post, not a board. Don't assume all posts are solid, or that all tie rings are solid — many aren't, so check them before tying to them. It's best to tie only to something designed for that purpose. Even then, be skeptical.

6. If you tie to a hitching rail, make sure it is high enough (at the horse's eye level) and solid and that the rope cannot slip over to the corner and down one side to the ground. The horse surely will pull it there if he can. The hitching rail should be five feet high, with a second bar lower so that the horse can't go under it. Ponies should be tied according to the same guidelines, but only to places suitable for ponies. They can slip under most horse hitching rails, gates, and holes in the fence. If you have ponies, you must build appropriate places to tie, groom, and bathe them.

7. Tie horses away from other horses and hazards that could cause them and the rope to become entangled, such as trees, branches, rocks, buckets, hay carts, nets, other trailers, wagons, farm implements, and hoses.

8. Tie only to a trailer that is hitched to a vehicle, especially the two-horse, bumper-pull variety. A big horse who panics or is enraged because he has been stung by a bee can move even a large trailer. At a minimum, he may seriously damage the trailer hitch. More important, he could hurt himself or, worse, a person.

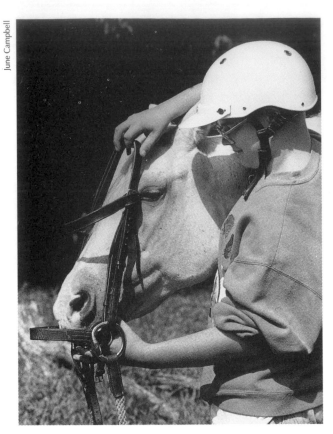

Stand to the side when bridling. This will prevent collisions between your head and the horse's.

June Campbell

9. If you tie to the tie ring of a trailer, check the under carriage of the trailer for sharp bare metal edges. If you find them, do not tie the horse there. If the horse paws or kicks a fly, he may turn sideways to do it and catch his foot under the trailer. Bare metal edges can sever a tendon, ligament, or a whole foot.

10. Do not leave a horse unattended at the trailer. This is a common horse show practice, and it's a bad one. A horse could injure himself or kick an unsuspecting spectator. This also is one of many reasons children should not be allowed to mill around unsupervised at a show where horses are tied to trailers.

11. If the horse must be tied to the trailer, tie him securely with a quick-release knot and an unbreakable halter. If he gets loose, he could injure someone or cause an accident. Better that he hurt himself rather than a person.

12. Do not leave a horse tied in a motionless trailer longer than it takes to get fuel unless you know for a fact that a horse is a seasoned traveler who will accept standing in a stationary trailer. Some horses are claustrophobic and will panic in a motionless trailer. (Some will panic in a moving trailer, too.)

Rules for Bridling

1. When you unfasten the halter, refasten it back around the horse's neck, even if you are holding the lead. This will provide more control than will reins over his neck and can be helpful when learning to bridle. As a general practice, it is better to untie the lead from the rail before bridling.

2. Stand back and beside the head to bridle so that the horse won't bang you with his own head. Do not stand in front of the horse's chest or under his head. Remember, never stand in front of the horse's feet.

3. Check your bridle before riding to be sure it is comfortable for the horse and be certain that it has no weak points — stretched places, tears, or bad stitching. It should be well oiled and supple if it is leather, and clean and well stitched if made of synthetic material.

4. Open the horse's mouth by placing your left thumb on the bars (where there are no teeth) and pressing down until the horse opens his mouth, then gently pull the bit into the mouth with your right hand and slip the crown piece over the ears. If you put your thumb too far back or forward…chomp, chomp!

Rules for Saddling

1. Check the saddle and pad for anything that could cause a sore. A horse with a back lesion could send the rider into an unintentional flying dismount.

2. Make an air passage under the pad, over the spine, by pulling the pad or blankets up into the gullet of the saddle. This keeps the saddle from drawing the pads tight across the withers later, which causes back soreness.

3. Place saddle and pads too far forward at first, then settle them back into place, moving the pad and saddle in the direction the hair grows. If you pull them forward against the hair, you can cause a sore place.

4. If you use Western tack, fasten the front cinch first, rear cinch last. Do the opposite when unsaddling. The main cinch is the only thing that will keep the saddle from turning. Always hook it first and unhook it last.

5. There must be a strap connecting the two cinches, and it must be secure to prevent the rear cinch from sliding back into the flank.

6. On Western saddles, tie-downs usually are snapped to the breast collar or to the cinch. Tie-downs and breast collars are completely fastened after the cinches are tightened and are removed before the cinches are unfastened, back cinch first.

7. English martingales and some English breast collars must be attached by running the girth through a loop on one end. Fasten the girth with martingale first and unfasten it last. Avoid attempting to remove a saddle that's still fastened to your horse by a martingale.

8. Secure the cinches and off stirrups up over the saddle horn to avoid banging the horse's belly or legs when swinging the saddle up. Lift or swing the Western saddle up and gently set it on the horse's back. Go around and let the cinches and stirrups down while checking the off side. Don't just drop them and let them bang the horse.

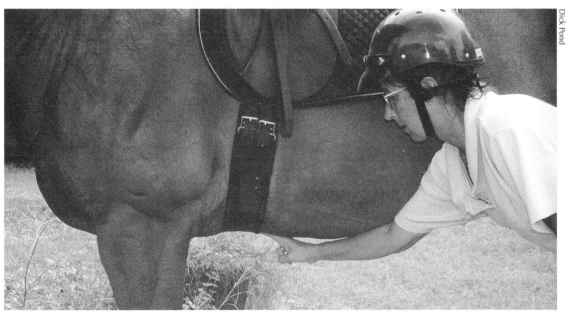

The girth or cinch should be checked at least three times. Check by inserting fingers from back to front so hair returns to normal when fingers are removed.

9. The back cinch should touch the horse's belly, so that neither a foot nor a twig can get underneath. But it should not be tight; remember, the rear cinch is to keep the back of the saddle down, not to keep the saddle on the horse.

10. Cinch or girth up the horse in stages so he will not get in the habit of bloating.

11. Instructors, wranglers, and trail guides must check all cinches and girths personally at least three times — before mounting, immediately after, and 10 to 15 minutes into the ride — by putting two fingers under the girth or cinch at the middle of the belly, back to front. The latter is to return the hair to normal when the fingers are removed. One finger means the girth or cinch is too tight; three fingers means it's too loose.

Rules for Mounting and Dismounting

1. Mount your horse in the open, away from fences and trees; never mount in the barn or near vehicles, horse walkers, or other obstacles.

2. A rider should seat herself gently in the saddle and ask the horse to stand quietly for several seconds after mounting, so he won't get the idea that getting on means "giddy-up go."

3. The rider's foot should be parallel to the horse or the toe in the girth or cinch, not in the horse, while mounting.

4. In addition to checking the girth before a student mounts, **remember** to check it two more times: right after the student has mounted and 10 to 15 minutes into the ride. Check it every time any student mounts, when there is a change of rider, or when the same rider is remounting.

5. Some saddles constructed of man-made materials may compress after mounting, loosening the cinch or girth and making it imperative that the cinch or girth be retightened immediately after mounting.

6. English riders should immediately "run up" their stirrups after dismounting so the irons won't be a swinging hazard. They can hit the rider or the horse and get caught on things.

7. After dismounting, all riders should immediately bring the reins over the horse's head for leading: closed reins, romal reins, buckled reins, double reins — all reins.

Rules for Arena Etiquette — the Warm-Up Area

1. Horses tracking left have the right-of-way, always.

2. Slow-moving horses leave the rail to faster horses.

3. Horses not on the rail pass left shoulder to left shoulder when possible.

4. Always look behind you before stopping and/or backing.

5. Minors should be supervised by someone knowledgeable — a trainer, parents, or club leader.

6. Experienced adults and older teens must watch out for adult novices and little ones.

7. Warm-up areas should have posted rules. A supervisor who reports to show

management should monitor the activities to protect not only the competitors but also the show management and the facility. This supervisor should be well informed about safety concerns. Safety certification is recommended.

Rules for Trail Riding

1. Students should be supervised when trail riding.
2. Trail riding should be permitted only if students or customers can demonstrate proper control and thorough knowledge of emergency procedures, such as the emergency stop. Optimally, a skills test should be required of anyone who wants to participate. (A skills test also can help prevent arguments with angry parents who want their child to trail ride but don't realize the child may not have adequate skills.)
3. Trails should be well maintained and not hazardous.
4. An alternate route should be provided around obstacles or jumps that are suitable only for advanced riders.
5. All school horses should be familiar with the trails before being assigned to a student. The instructor, not the students, should train the horses.
6. All horses on trail rides should wear halters with lead ropes for emergencies.
7. There should be one guide for every six students and never fewer than two guides, unless the guide can communicate with the barn by cellular phone or radio, and the riders are at least at the intermediate level. It is nearly impossible to see more than six riders ahead. This means 12 students require three guides or one instructor and two guides. The sequence with a dozen students is:

Instructor   *Students*   *Guide*   *Students*   *Guide*

8. Always wait for a dismounted rider, or any lagging rider.
9. The level of difficulty and speed should be gauged to the least proficient rider.
10. Always stop and wait for the rear guide to close the gate. (See Rule 8.)
11. If it's hunting season and there's any chance that hunters could be in the woods where you usually trail ride, don't trail ride.
12. Don't take out a ride in bad or threatening weather.
13. If you get caught in really bad weather — lightning, hail, ice — dismount the ride and tie the horses, or, if you are riding in an area where horses won't have to cross roads to get home, take off their bridles and send them along.
14. Before each trail lesson, review emergency procedures including those for:
    - Falls
    - Bad weather
    - Illness
15. Never ride when there is lightning. Get everyone off their horses and to a low place away from trees.

16. Know the trails and do not explore.
17. Never assume you can dismount all riders and lead them through a difficult area. Sometimes, it is more dangerous to lead than to ride.
18. Be sure riders maintain proper spacing at all times. Each rider should see the feet of the horse ahead between the ears of his own horse. If he sees only the hocks it is a warning; if he sees the tail, it's a problem.
19. Never permit anyone to pass the lead instructor or wrangler unless it's a staff member sent forward on a mission.

Rules for Trailering/Hauling

1. Check hitch, bumper, lights, brakes, and tires, including spares, on truck and trailer before each trip. Locate the jack, jack handle, and lug wrench for both truck and trailer.
2. Check the trailer floor before each trip; if wood, it should be treated to make it more rot resistant.
3. Tie horses short in the trailer so that their heads cannot go below their chests or back to their shoulders.
4. Try always to use shipping boots. When hauling more than one horse, boots are mandatory to avoid injuries caused by horses stepping on each other.
5. Always untie the horse before lowering the tailgate or opening the rear door. If you must enter a trailer to do this (we hope not!), have someone else man the door.
6. It is better to have two people for hauling, but it is especially helpful for loading and unloading.
7. Never leave horses unattended at or in a trailer.
8. Recognize that the ride in the trailer is different from the one in the truck, and drive accordingly. Accelerate *only after* a turn and then only when the trailer is straight behind the vehicle; avoid weaving among lanes. Remember, the horse doesn't have arms to stabilize himself by bracing against the trailer walls. He can only lean his body, which is tiring and can be scary.
9. When possible, get the horse out of the trailer for exercise at regular intervals, such as every four to five hours. Avoid hauling horses for more than 12 hours a day unless they have had an overnight rest.
10. Watch the weather as a pilot would. If driving is hazardous in a car, it is worse with a trailer. Trying to get horses off the road — or to keep a horse trailer on the road — in a storm or blizzard can be a nightmare.
11. Whenever possible, carry cellular phones. Cellular phones are great. There are far fewer cellular "dead spots" than there used to be on the highways, except in mountainous areas.
12. Teach horses to load by themselves so that a handler does not need to risk walking in a two-horse trailer with them. Teaching a horse to load by himself also teaches him to back out. Sometimes it is necessary to unload unexpectedly; a horse that will not reload by himself is a serious problem under those circumstances.
13. In many new slant-load trailers, tie rings are provided inside and out. It still

is better to tie a horse *outside*. This is especially important in a stock trailer to avoid having to squeeze in beside the horses. Stay out of closed, tight places with horses whenever you can.

14. Avoid unloading onto pavement because the horse can easily slip.
15. Carry reflective markers or flares in case of a breakdown.
16. Always travel prepared for a breakdown. This also means with horses loaded so they can stand awhile if necessary; that is, the trailer must fit the horses; horses should have hay; should have had regular exercise during the trip; and wear shipping boots to protect restless legs. There should be a rubber mat on the floor. If you can, also put down about three to six inches of shavings as an added cushion.

The one time you leave something out is the one time you will be stuck on the side of the road that has no shoulder, with heavy traffic, and barbed wire on both sides. You'll be alone, and your horses will already have been in the trailer, unwrapped, for nine hours. Now you are in it up to your armpits and sinking deeper.

Rules for the Facility

1. Keep barn aisles free of tools, tack, and trunks. Store trash cans elsewhere.
2. Stall doors should open outward or, preferably, slide.
3. In areas where horses are permitted, make sure there is nothing that could catch on a halter, saddle, or bridle.
4. Large signs should direct people to knock or whistle before entering a horse area, prohibit smoking, and notify visitors of barn safety rules.
5. Roll or coil water hoses out of the way after each use. Hoses lying around can spook or trip a horse or trip a person leading a horse, which may then cause the horse to spook.
6. Make sure electrical cords are out of reach of horses and their curious mouths.
7. Most barn aisles are 12 feet wide, too narrow to permit walking around the horse without walking into the horse's space or comfort zone. Approach each horse tied in the aisle individually at the shoulder.
8. Construct arena fencing and gates so that riders' toes and knees won't catch on them.
9. Riding areas must have gates that close when riders are inside.
10. Cross-country and pasture riding are not for novice students. Post warning signs to that effect.
11. Never, ever ride into or in the barn.
12. Park all vehicles well away from areas where horses and people come together.
13. Horses should be led from the barn to the riding area and back.
14. Aisleways should be dirt or a nonslip material.
15. Provide adequate, solid hitching rails in the tacking-up area.
16. Tacking-up stalls should have a safe escape route for people. Such stalls should not be used by novices without supervision. This is no place for students and horses to be alone. Convenient as they are, they can be traps for the inexperienced if a horse spooks or panics.

17. Anywhere horses and people come together must have plenty of room to maneuver — a minimum of 12 feet by 12 feet. Consider this when planning tacking-up areas.
18. Do not permit riding in the following areas and situations:
    - Any area containing loose horses
    - Any area where horses are tied — this requires a rule that horses are not to be tied in a riding ring, arena, or any other area where horses are ridden — *ever*
    - Any area with a serious hazard, such as a horse walker not protected by a fence
    - Any area currently under construction or where workmen and/or heavy equipment are present
    - Anywhere that farm equipment is stored
    - Any area open to a highway or main road

The facility rules should require that riding be permitted only in areas designated for that purpose. Check those areas regularly and thoroughly for safety.

Rules for Fences and Gates

1. A fence and a closed gate should enclose the entire facility.
2. No loose horse or ridden horse that is out of control should be able to make its way to a public road.

1. Wear your _____ whenever you are working around horses or riding them. (page 6)

2. A horse's kicking range (or comfort zone) is _____ feet or more. (page 6)

3. Who should ride each new lesson or trail horse first? (page 6)

4. A rule for tying is _____ high and_____ length. (page 11)

5. Place these items in the order they are (a) fastened and (b) unfastened: back cinch, martingale or tie-down, breast collar, front cinch. (page 13)

6. The instructor must check all cinches or girths _____times. (page 14)

7. The handler should pass through a gate or door (before, after, or at the same time) as the horse. (page 10)

8. Horses tracking in which direction have the right-of-way? (page 14)

9. There should be no more than _____ students between wranglers or instructors on a trail ride. (page 15)

10. True or False: Accelerate after a turn only when the trailer is straight behind the vehicle. (page 16)

THE NATURE
OF THE HORSE

The following information should always be your first lesson with any new student.

If the student is a minor, it is wise to have at least one parent present so that everybody understands that safety comes first and is the principal current running throughout all lessons.

This is a good time to go over release forms and to hand out and review stable rules and requirements for attire, promptness, cancellations, method of payment, medical consent forms, and emergency procedures. All should be in writing, but many people won't read the material unless it's reviewed with them. Do this personally, not by means of videotape, so you can be sure that everything is understood. This also is an opportunity to avoid some problems that would remain in the background without open discussion of rules and policies. You'll be glad you took the extra time.

During this safety lesson, the instructor begins to build a perception of the horse in the minds of the students that underscores their need to take precautions. Learning to handle and ride horses then will have a logical foundation that is more easily remembered. All lessons have their roots here.

Even if one were the greatest horse trainer ever, there is still one thing that she/he cannot train the horse to do. No one can train the horse not to be a horse. Even with the most well-trained horse on the planet, under a certain amount of physical and/or mental pressure the training goes out the window, and the horse is still a horse. He is fundamentally a big, powerful animal who looks out for his own interests. So, we as horsemen must understand this animal and deal with him in terms he can understand. We must learn what he is and accept what he is because we cannot change what he is.

Through time, the horse, as well as other grazing animals of the plains, has been motivated by three instincts:

1. The urge to reproduce and have many offspring
2. The urge to live long enough to accomplish the first — or with geldings, a will to live — although by now they've forgotten why
3. The urge to stay with a group for mutual protection ("maybe the wolf will eat him, not me")

For the sake of discussion, suppose we had a snarling, savage, man-eating stallion; a spirited jumper; and Old Dobbin, the 22-year-old school horse. Which horse is statistically most likely to cause an accident or hurt someone? If you guessed Old Dobbin, you're right. People forget that he is still a horse; they take him for granted and are careless. They will not be careless with the first two. Just knowing about horses is not enough. You must respect them as well — all of them.

A. The Horse's Greatest Fear

There are two groups of animals: predators and prey. The horse is a prey animal. He belongs to the group that is eaten by the other group — the predators. The greatest threat to a horse in the wild was that a predator would eat him, and these instincts are still there.

Only those horses physically and mentally adapted to evading predators, such as wolves, bears, and wild hogs, lived long enough to have a lot of babies. This means that only those characteristics that helped the horse stay alive, or that at least were not detrimental, were passed on to the young. Characteristics of the horse that hindered his escape wouldn't have been passed on, because that horse wouldn't have escaped, and he would have had no young because he would have been eaten. We, not nature, are responsible for breeding some calm, gentle horses that seem to accept a lot of commotion. We must recognize that some horses seem to accept a lot of commotion. Also, some horses considered to be difficult could be the ones with the most highly developed survival skills.

Of course, humans are the supreme predators. Once this one fact is understood, we must do everything around the horse in a manner designed to convince the horse we do not intend to harm him or, more specifically, to eat him.

B. Characteristics That Protect the Horse

The evolution of horses has equipped them, to a certain extent, against predators. Consider the following characteristics:

Wide-set eyes. These give the horse good peripheral vision so he can see the predator sneaking up from behind.

Powerful hind legs. Well-developed, muscular hindquarters allow the horse to escape quickly or defend against attackers.

Acute hearing. This perhaps is the horse's best sense and most important defensive weapon against predators.

Sense of smell. The horse's acute sense of smell helps detect predators, unsavory feeds, and other dangers; it also helps direct the horse to safe, familiar territory — the first of which is its mother's flank.

Big teeth and an even bite. These are not only efficient for eating, but they are also good fighting weapons.

Free shoulders. These allow the front legs to strike, stomp, and run.

Herd instinct. This tells horses to remain in the group — the wolf can't eat all of them, and they know it.

C. What Makes the Horse Want to Flee or Fight

The approach of a predator or the suspicion of a predator is the main cause of flight. If you are a prey animal like the horse, you must assume anything sudden or strange is a predator. Unknown or sudden noises or movements may signal the approach of a predator, and you don't want to wait around to make sure. Generally, horses prefer to flee if they can and will only fight if they must. Keep this in mind when you catch a horse.

What exactly is a predator? Predators can be *carnivores*, that is, meat-eating animals that kill and eat other animals (lions, tigers, and wolves), or they can be *omnivores*, that is, animals that kill and eat other animals but also eat leaves, nuts, berries, and other vegetable matter as a regular part of their diet (bears, pigs, and humans). A horse will put anything strange in the predator category until he has reason not to. From the beginning, we are in the wrong group, and somehow we must change the horse's mind.

The horse that survived was not the horse who took chances with the unknown. If something looked, smelled, or sounded strange, it must have been a predator and, therefore, must have been dangerous.

Prey animals are herbivores (grazers and browsers), like cows, giraffes, and horses. (We will leave out birds and fish.)

Carnivores smell different from herbivores. What does your breath smell like after a burger? A vegetarian will not have the same odor as those of us who eat meat.

Animals know the scents of other animals and react accordingly. Horses can be terrified of the scent of a bear, whether or not they have ever seen one, yet be only mildly afraid of the unfamiliar smell of a cow, for example. This is instinctive. The horse who was repelled by the scent of a predator was the one who got away.

Let's look at the horse tied up in the barn. He is caught, restrained, and has every reason to be terrified. We ask a lot of the horse to allow us to do anything at all, but it is extremely important that we understand first and foremost that we were, and sometimes are, predators to the horse. He cannot help that initial response, and he will, without doubt, revert to it under pressure. It is vital that we not startle or threaten the horse. He must have the confidence that we mean him no harm. If we betray this, he again will group us with the other predators. He must trust us.

D. Overcoming the Flee/Fight Reflex

Because we know how the horse perceives the world, we also know what we have to do to enable the horse to feel safe. We must not appear to have predator habits so that we may teach the horse to respond otherwise and to override his survival instincts.

The horse must know **who we are, where we are, and what we are doing.**

Who we are: All the horse cares about is that we are not a predator. To tell him that, we must tell him we are something else by avoiding predator like mannerisms and habits.

Where we are: When we announce our presence to a horse and keep him informed of where we are, we separate ourselves from other predators. They don't announce themselves, especially if they are hungry.

What we are doing: The horse wants to know that we don't plan to eat him. We cannot just say, "Blaze, I'm not going to eat you." We must communicate this by letting the horse first know who we are and where we are, and then by indicating another intention such as running a hand down the horse's leg — "I'm going to clean your hoof." You are telling the horse: (Who) "I am not a predator; (Where) you know I'm here by your shoulder; (What) I'm going to clean your hoof."

We must approach the horse in a manner that is non threatening. The horse must be able to hear us and see us, and not worry about what we are going to do. Well, that sounds easy, but often we do this incorrectly without knowing it. Let's see how predators approach him, and then we won't do it that way.

What part of the horse would a predator approach? A predator might sneak up behind him and bite his leg, damaging tendons so that he can't run. A predator might run up to the horse's neck and slash the veins. If the predators are wolves, which will attack an old or young or sick horse, one might grab the horse at the nose and wait for the rest of the pack to move in for the kill.

What do we learn from this? We don't go to the horse's hind legs, or his neck, or his face. We go up to his shoulder, walking normally, talking normally. No predator walks up, making noise, to the one part of the horse where he can't get a good bite or a firm hold. Predators approach by walking softly and making little noise. Sound familiar? Many of us were taught to walk up to a horse slowly and to talk softly. Now we know better — walk normally, talk normally — do not shout or run.

We tell the horse where we are with our voice and touch and by staying in his sight. We know he hears us because we watch his ears. If his ears don't register our voice by moving, we don't approach. The horse must acknowledge our presence. Of course, he may turn and look at us, which is even better. If he turns his rump to us, we know he is not convinced, so we wait until he turns. We don't go up to a horse who has turned his rump toward us, not ever. Remember we are talking to students or customers, not to the veterinarian or farrier. Sometimes, we have to work around this, for instance, to give medication.

When the horse acknowledges our presence with his ears or by turning and looking, we continue talking and walk up and stroke his shoulder — stroke, not tickle or slap.

As we move around the horse, we continue talking, and we keep a hand on

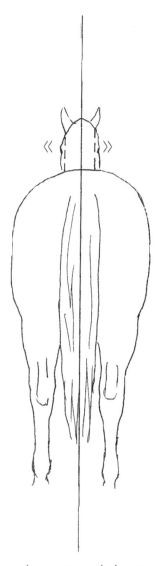

Even the most gentle horse will keep you in view with slight movements of his head from side to side.

him. When we walk behind the horse, our hand and arm go around his hindquarters, touching them before we step from one side to the other. If he is going to kick, let him kick when only the arm is back there.

We never stop directly behind the horse. This is a real "never." Staying in the horse's view is safer. Because the horse's eyes are set on the side of his head, he can see down his sides. He cannot see directly behind his rump or directly in front of his head. These are his blind spots. In fact, if you step back and forth behind a horse, talking and with a hand always on his rump, most horses will follow your voice with their ears and keep you in view with slight movements of their head from side to side. Even the most gentle horse will do this, which tells us how important our location is to every horse.

We let the horse know what we are doing by giving him plenty of warning. When we pick up a hoof, we always run a hand calmly down the leg of the hoof we wish to lift. We don't just grab the foot.

Who we are. Where we are. What we are doing.

In all movements around the horse we must be calm and confident like his trusted friend, not sneaky and sudden like the wolf.

Remember, a tied-up horse may doze while being groomed. Keep him awake by talking and by touching him. If you move away you must reintroduce yourself. Failure to reintroduce is a common cause of accidents and near-accidents.

E. How the Horse Likes to Be Touched

Stroke don't pat. The foal's earliest memory is of its mother's tongue gently licking and cleaning. As the foal grows, she continues to lick and nuzzle her baby. She does not slap him or pat him. She will nip and butt to discipline. Stroking a horse connects to the animal's earliest memory.

Do you remember ever hitting your head on a kitchen cabinet or being hit in the head? Do you recall someone uninvited adjusting your collar or fiddling with your hair? Try walking up to someone, even a friend, and putting your hand in his face. He won't like it. Have someone put his hand in your face. It's not pleasant; in fact, it's annoying. A blow to the head usually makes us angry, while bumping a chair with an arm would not.

Horses feel the same way about their heads and faces. This area of the body houses the brain. We instinctively protect this area. Horses do, too. They prefer a gentle, calm touch that they know is coming, not a tickle or a "butterfly's wing."

F. A Horse Is a Herd Animal

The horse must learn to perform away from a group. He does not do this by choice. His instinct tells him that there is safety in numbers. The lone grazing animal often was eaten. This is why we don't get separated on the trail, why we don't ride out alone, and why we have the quiet, calm horse at the head of the line, and why we don't pass the leader on the trail. The horse in the lead position is the most likely to be startled, so the horse in this position needs to be the least likely to spook.

As you gain experience, you will learn to give your horse confidence when you ride him, but you must understand that the horse will always prefer to stay with a group or back at the barn, because that's where he feels safe. Training and experience will teach a horse to gain confidence from his rider, just as he does from his handler on the ground. Your legs must give the same confidence while mounted that your hands do while on the ground.

G. A Word About Response

Begin talking about response with your students in the first ground lesson — then it won't come as any surprise later on.

There are many schools of thought regarding horsemanship. We subscribe to the principle that the comfortable, unworried horse is a safe horse. We also believe that the fearful or uncomfortable horse is a dangerous horse. This doesn't mean that we let the horse have his own way, but that our communications with the horse are within his level of tolerance and make sense to him.

We must recognize that the horse needs *consistency* and that he cannot tolerate *frustration*. Our behavior around and on the horse must be compatible with this "nature of the horse," because we cannot change what he is.

Response and the Ridden Horse

We have all heard about the "dead-sided" horse. Yet that same animal will feel a fly land on his skin. How do we explain this phenomenon?

Horses learn conditioned response. It all begins with pressure. The horse can respond only to pressure. You press with your leg, the horse moves; you pull the reins, the horse stops. He is motivated to do this in order to make the pressure go away.

We begin to talk about pressure on the ground. We ask the horse to move over. We push until we feel his weight shift. We release and push again. Finally, the horse takes one step. We do not follow and keep pushing; instead, we repeat the process using lighter and lighter pressure until the horse will move over from our fingertips: touch, push, step, release, touch, push, step, release.

If we kept pushing instead of releasing and pushing again, the horse would have

Mares lick and nuzzle their foals. They do not slap or pat their babies. That's why it's better for us to stroke, not pat, a horse, because stroking will link to the horse's earliest memory.

no reason to take the second step, since the first step got him nowhere. The horse responds only to release of the pressure. He isn't trying to find out what we want; he simply feels something, and he moves or responds away from the pressure. If we do not understand this when we are on him, we will have a horse that you can kick all day and still get nowhere and who "needs spurs." Yet the horse simply has decided that moving won't remove the pressure, so if he can, he tunes it out or *ignores* it.

If the horse moves at all, anywhere, he must be given credit for answering the rider. When the handler or rider gets an unexpected response, he must look again at where and how the pressure was applied. For example, was the leg in the correct place? The rider still rewards because he asked, and the horse responded; the rider just didn't ask very well.

At the highest levels of riding, the horse still is only responding with his body to a sophisticated, coordinated set of pressures. Beginners can just as easily adopt this philosophy as others, and this one won't ruin or sour your horses. Teach the beginners to ask again, not punish. This doesn't mean the horse will be spoiled, only that he will be ridden in a more refined or sophisticated manner, depending on the level of the rider. Children use sophisticated computers every day; they can learn to ride correctly and humanely just as easily as they can master a computer game, assuming the motivation is there. That's the instructor's job.

In a nutshell, horses do not reason; they learn conditioned response through habitual behavior. They probably cannot connect two events more than a few seconds apart unless the events themselves are connected in some way. For example, the horse bites and gets spanked. If he gets spanked several minutes after he bites, he won't know why he got spanked. All he knows is someone hit him for no reason — there goes the trust.

The horse can make associations. You ride down the road, and the horse spooks at a bicycle at the end of the lane and gets a spanking. The next time the horse sees a bicycle, he may spook because he fears the spanking. This is association.

If he spooks and gets his spanking every time that he comes to the end of the lane, soon he will act up and "spook" before he gets to the end of the lane, because he knows where he'll get the spanking. That is anticipation. If you let him look around at the end of the lane, and reassure him instead of punishing him for being afraid, he'll be less likely to spook.

Sometimes, the show horse will anticipate by connecting the announcer's words to the expected response. Other horses may associate a location, an odor, or a sight with an event. Horses cannot reason, but they can be quite clever in connecting events and actions.

We must understand response to pressure, habit, association, and anticipation so that we can use the nature of the horse toward positive, safe ends.

Chapter 2 — Review Questions

1. What is the horse's greatest fear? (page 21)

2. Who is the supreme predator? (page 21)

3. Name four characteristics that protect the horse. (pages 21-22)

4. Unless we convince a horse otherwise, to him we are more like (a) cows, or (b) bears. (page 22)

5. What three things must we always let the horse know so that we do not threaten him? (page 23)

6. Name three places on the horse where a lone predator will attack. (page 23)

7. A dead-sided or hard-mouthed horse results when the horse is conditioned to _____ pressure. (page 25)

8. If the horse moves in response to pressure, you should give him credit by applying _____ pressure. (pages 25-26)

9. The application of all aids or cues can be explained as rewarding the horse with a _____ whenever he responds to_____. (page 26)

10. We must understand response to pressure, _____, _____, and _____ if we want to use the horse's own nature to achieve positive safe ends. (page 26)

HORSEMANSHIP: WESTERN OR ENGLISH?

Although this handbook may seem to emphasize English horsemanship, the AAHS does not favor or promote one style over the other. To a certain extent, we do favor starting beginners in English saddles to remove the temptation to grab and hold on to the saddle horn. Also, in the event of a fall, it is unlikely that the rider or the rider's clothing will hang up on an English saddle, increasing the severity of the fall. The rider will fall clear. The Western saddle may give beginners a false sense of security, making them feel less likely to fall off. We also start all riders two-handed to keep the upper body square and more easily balanced.

In many respects, *correct* Western riding is more difficult because Western riders must be able to demonstrate the same skills as English riders, but with only one hand on the reins and with a much lighter contact with the horse's mouth. Yes, there can be "contact" on a loose rein. The horse still is "on the bit" or "on the aids." The basic aids are the same, although most Western riders use the term "cues."

A. An Essay for All Riders

It should be possible to draw a line perpendicular to the horizon from the rider's ear to his shoulder to the point of the hip to the back of the heel. A good Western equitation rider still should be able to stand in his stirrups at any time, at any gait, without moving his feet. In fact, I first saw that exercise done, including the rising trot, in a nationally known Western barn.

The terminology is different. The Western horse walks, jogs, and lopes, but those gaits are the same, in principle, as the walk, trot, and canter. Only their style and movement vary. Some parts of Western tack are different in appearance, but the same parts are called by the same names. Western saddles have some parts that are not present on an English saddle.

Bad horsemanship is just that: bad horsemanship. A bad Western rider is no worse than a bad English rider. A good English rider is no better than a good Western rider.

Thanks to Hollywood, we have grown up with an unfortunate idea of Western horsemanship. We see, especially in the older movies, many examples of jerking hands, bouncing bodies, horses tied by their reins (sometimes all night!). We see horses tied to the back of a moving vehicle, or falling tail over teakettle down a rocky incline, maybe even followed down the hill by a stagecoach.

Those were the days before humane societies started monitoring the treatment of animals on movie lots. Unfortunately, even today, not every actor who is on a horse in a Western movie can ride a horse. Bad horsemanship in films makes good Western riders cringe as much as it does good English riders.

The problem is that generations of kids have grown up thinking that this is riding, and that movies like City Slickers are reality. Then they go to a stable or summer camp wanting to do the same.

We seldom see on the silver screen a picture featuring a true hackamore reinsman or that cowboy who rode his ranch's rough stock and "just had a way with horses." A good Western rider is just as poetic on his cow pony, reiner, or cutting horse as an English rider on his dressage horse, Grand Prix jumper, or hunter.

Whatever the style, if the horse and rider do not appear to be a harmonious unit, it probably is bad riding. The really great Western riders of our time, Ray Hunt, Jack Kyle, Monte Foreman, Matlock Rose, Jackie Krshka, to name a few, would be great riders no matter what saddle they were sitting in. The really great English riders also would manage very nicely in any saddle.

The point is that all normal horses have four legs that move in a limited number of sequences: walk, trot, or jog, canter or lope, slow gait, rack, pace, and some other four-beat variations. The center of gravity is the same and reacts in the same way to changes in speed and degree of collection.

Archive Photos

Riding as portrayed in many Hollywood films has not set a good example, especially for safety.

Until they take away a leg or add a fifth one, there really is only one way to sit on this animal and be in harmony with his movements, whether you are riding English, Western, or sidesaddle.

B. The Basic Seat

In all forms of riding, whether Western or English, the basic seat is the same with only slight variations, and even these are dictated more by whether the rider is holding the reins evenly in one hand or in both.

The Basic Seat
- The rider sits upright.
- The body is aligned with the ear, shoulder, point of the hip, and back of the heel on a vertical line perpendicular to the horizon.
- The eyes are forward, not down.
- The back is straight and flat.
- The seat bones are planted firmly in the deepest part of the saddle.
- The legs are straight down, not out in front.
- The ball of the foot is on the stirrup.
- The toe is pointed up, with the heel down.

Slight Variations for the Single-Handed Rider
- The rein hand is carried in the middle with special care taken not to allow the one-handed style to cause the rider to tilt the shoulder of the rein hand forward. This applies to Western riders, polo players, and cavalry-style riders.
- The free hand is carried in a relaxed manner straight down at the rider's side, or the rider may hold the excess reins with the free hand.
- The free hand may be used to carry and swing the polo mallet.
- In Mexican-style, sidesaddle riding, the free hand holds the butt of the riding whip, which lies across the lower arm near the elbow of the rein hand.

Traditionally, the left hand is the preferred rein hand, which probably stems from the days when the right hand was kept free to wield a saber

The basic seat is the same, whether the rider is riding hunt seat, saddle seat, or Western style.

or pistol. It should be noted that Native Americans did not have such formal constraints about riding.

In Western showing, horses that are 5 years old and younger, which are called "junior" horses, may be ridden two-handed in a snaffle bit, bosal, or side-pull. This has led many Western instructors to teach beginners to ride with two hands — an admirable quality if one really wants to produce a balanced rider. Starting riders with two hands on the reins recognizes the fact that it takes several years to teach a horse to neck-rein properly and also to teach a student to keep his horse together with one hand.

Sidesaddle differs in that the rider has both legs on the same side of the horse. However, an accomplished sidesaddle rider will have both seat bones squarely placed, evenly, in the deepest part of the saddle. Her shoulders will be square, and her reins will be held evenly whether she is riding English style with two hands, or Mexican or Western style with one hand.

1. The body alignment for Western riding is different for English riding or the same? (page 30)

2. True or False: With Western or English riding, it should be possible to draw a line perpendicular to the horizon from the rider's ear to his shoulder to the point of the hip to the back of the heel. (page 28)

3. With all forms of riding, where should the eyes look? (page 30)

4. How is the back held? (page 30)

5. Where are the seat bones planted? (page 30)

6. What part of the foot is on the stirrup? (page 30)

7. What direction should the toe be pointed? (page 30)

8. Where should the heel be? (page 30)

9. For the single-handed Western rider, where does the free hand go? (page 30)

10. In Mexican-style, sidesaddle riding, the free hand holds what? (page 30)

QUALITIES OF AN EFFECTIVE INSTRUCTOR

Becoming an effective instructor is no easy task. Multiple skills must be mastered, incorporated, and conveyed to students, who have different riding abilities and goals. As we've said before in this manual, a dedicated instructor of average talent can learn to be an excellent instructor through thoughtful study and practice.

A. The Effective Instructor:

Here we have summed up the qualities of an effective instructor. She:
1. Considers the safety of her students above all else.
2. Has a plan for each lesson, but is flexible if the situation requires an adjustment.
3. Has plans that interrelate.
4. Considers the age and educational background of the students and teaches accordingly. She never talks down to students. (She remembers how early kids learn about computers.)
5. Assumes that the students know little about correct horsemanship; if they do, they will advance quickly, and the instructor will know that nothing has been omitted.
6. Uses examples and personal experiences in teaching.
7. Explains words and terms that must be used.
8. Does not talk longer than five minutes without involving the students in some manner, unless it is a ground school class.
9. Initiates discussion, but keeps it *time-controlled*.
10. Gauges effectiveness by student expression and participation.
11. Whenever possible, keeps all students busy, even when working with an individual. This can be effective practice time for other students.

12. Wears neat and proper attire. This means correct riding clothes for her type of riding or neat casual clothes; no jogging shorts or sweats, please. Riding clothes are preferred because she should be prepared to demonstrate the skills herself on horseback.

13. Has good voice projection and uses correct language, no swear words or street slang. Don't say, "Canter, dudes," unless it's that kind of ranch.

14. Maintains eye contact with students; leaves no students out.

15. Exhibits a helpful attitude; respects all questions and problems.

16. Avoids sarcasm and ridicule, but uses humor effectively.

17. Is punctual and reliable.

18. Doesn't bluff, is ready to admit that she doesn't know, but adds, "I'll try to find out."

19. Doesn't embarrass students by criticizing their attire, but will explain the reason for correct attire. "It looks better" isn't a reason. Loose hair can impair vision; ill-fitting clothes can cause discomfort or even an accident.

20. Keeps an optimistic attitude concerning the students and horses.

21. Is patient, enthusiastic, friendly, and treats all students fairly.

22. Exhibits a professional attitude and knows her subject matter well. This means that she takes horsemanship seriously and continues to study by reading and taking lessons.

23. Maintains class control during lessons and especially in the event of an accident. Poor class control can cause many accidents.

24. Utilizes her assistant effectively in all situations. She should consider her assistant an apprentice and not assume experience that may not be there.

25. Seeks to learn each student's riding goal, whether it be pleasure riding, competition, or some other aim, and gear her instruction in those terms where possible: "Mary, even if you don't plan to show, it's helpful to be able to safely jump a log on the trail."

26. Finds out what the student already knows about horses and horsemanship, perhaps by examination or by starting with the basics and proceeding until she reaches the student's limit of competence.

The riding instructor should dress for riding. She may need to demonstrate a skill on a student's horse.

27. Keeps an attitude of helpfulness, empathy, and interest while seeking progress in each lesson.
28. Shows *enthusiasm*, as it can generate student enthusiasm. Humor and enthusiasm make the necessary repetitive exercises more fun. Anything can be competition. Anything can be a game. The student can only take out of the arena what the instructor brings into it.
29. Understands that students can learn and have fun at a tolerable level of risk. Students do not have to take risks to have fun. Make lessons fun by challenging the students at their skill level, by creating games, and giving prizes. (Adult students like prizes, too!) Gymnastic exercises help boost confidence.
30. *Considers the safety of her students above all else.*

Instructors must know whom not to teach. If the student is too young, inattentive, not interested, or simply not ready, no effective learning will take place. The gifted or highly dedicated instructor might create interest and enthusiasm where none existed before; however, most instructors are average — that's why it's called average.

We must be careful when mounting *fearful* or seriously *uninterested* students; they may be unwilling or unable to learn enough to be safe. Sometimes we must advise the parent to wait or perhaps to allow the student to participate in a sport that has more appeal for him. A good rule of thumb for a minimum age to begin riding lessons is 10 years old. It does not need to be a firm rule, only a starting place. You can make the occasional exception. Or you may choose to make the age younger but advise some parents to wait. Or you may deal with the needs of the very young. You do so at your own risk, as young children are especially vulnerable. You must have an appropriate facility and an appropriate pony for them.

Students young and old ride for a variety of reasons. Some may seek competition, but others may be drawn by the love of the animal, being outdoors, or the social aspect of participating in a fun activity. Still, while we may play games when learning to ride to help develop skills, learning to ride itself is not a game and must be taken seriously.

It is the responsibility of the instructor to hold the interest of the students to the degree necessary for them to learn the skills required to be safe and to see that they use those skills even when no one is watching.

B. The Learning Process: Repetition, Variety, Procedure, Repetition

Students learn best by seeing, hearing, saying, and doing. To learn effectively, students need to see it, hear about it, explain it, and do it. Students may even start a notebook in ground school sessions.

Encourage them to practice their riding skills on many different horses to promote better balance and feel. If the instructor is limited in the number of horses available, the lessons must be more creative to give the student variety and to teach different skills or the same skill in different situations. Students who learn skills as repeated procedures or steps are less likely to omit parts of a skill.

C. Feelings of Accomplishment

Students must experience a feeling of accomplishment after each lesson. They must feel that they are making progress. Remind them of their achievements every time they ride, even if the lesson is not entirely satisfactory. An effective instructor will back up and refine a previously learned skill if that's what it takes to end each lesson on a positive note.

Present lessons in such a way that students can perform the required skills with feelings of success. They must come away from each lesson with a new skill and an answer to the question, "What did you learn today?" If the student can't explain to the instructor (or parent) what he learned, the instructor did not teach the lesson effectively.

D. Student Factors That Hinder Learning

The student's age and mental and physical condition have an important bearing on progress. Preconceived ideas, shyness, fear, uncomfortable clothing, illness, fatigue, and distractions all hinder the learning process, as do growth spurts, puberty, and family problems. An ill-behaved student will not learn and will hinder others' learning. Ill-behaved students also pose a safety hazard, so use discretion as to whether to keep them in the class. If a student's attention cannot be refocused on the lesson, the instructor should excuse the student for the benefit and safety of the others.

E. Instructor Factors That Hinder Learning

Instructors should be alert to common teaching faults that hinder learning.

Some Common Teaching Faults:
- Talking too fast and too much, mostly too much. It is difficult to listen and do at the same time.
- Presenting material without enthusiasm, in a style that is too reserved or even boring.
- Making teaching seem like a chore, rather than a challenge and a pleasure.
- Displaying impatience or favoritism. Please, never favoritism.
- Talking too much about themselves and their experiences: "When I won the national championship" or "When I went to camp here."
- Failing to involve all the students in the lesson, or leaving them inactive too long.
- Not giving breaks in an hour-long lesson, to halt, walk, and observe others. Material is better absorbed if you allow small segments of time for thought.

In training the horse, we think in terms of a 15-minute warm-up, a 30-minute lesson, and a 15-minute cool down. This also works for people. Green horses and novice riders are learning.

F. Motivation and Learning

Most students want to learn to ride well in the shortest length of time. For the others, the instructor can use a number of techniques to motivate learning.

Techniques to Motivate Learning
- Arouse curiosity by hinting at what new skills will lead to
- Use praise and incentives
- Exhibit a positive teaching approach
- List the benefits of correct learning
- Make the student feel that the instructor has a genuine interest in him and his progress
- Encourage friendly competition in skill games. Skill games are easily made up for each lesson. How many times can you . . . ? How quickly . . . ?

If students understand the use of the skill being taught and what would happen if they lack the skill, most will be patient. With a little imagination, skill teaching can be fun for all. Knowing the skills and how they *interrelate* enables the instructor to tell where her students are in their learning — that is, what it is safe for them to do.

If a student seriously lacks motivation after several efforts, his attitude should be discussed with his parents, because a lack of interest will be a safety hazard for that student and for the rest of the class.

G. The Adult Student

The adult offers his own problems, not only in the area of motivation, but also in physical ability. Kids usually pick up new athletic skills quickly; their bodies are more supple, and they usually are less apprehensive. Equally important, kids are accustomed to taking instruction on a daily basis.

In contrast, the Type A, overzealous adult can be much more difficult to teach. The overachieving, adult professional may be accustomed to immediate success. "The harder I work, the better I do" may not apply to riding, since the extra, conscious effort may result in tension. An instructor needs to be aware of this. And all adults are not the same — the fit, amateur athlete will find riding fairly easy at the beginning; the couch potato will not.

An adult may have the attitude that all he wants to learn is to start, stop, and steer and will take some convincing that it is necessary to learn the basics — including balance and an independent seat through the walk, trot, and canter and low obstacles — to be safe enough to ride unsupervised, especially out of the arena. Some adults will also have unrealistically high goals and there, you just have to go with the flow and urge them to take each step in turn.

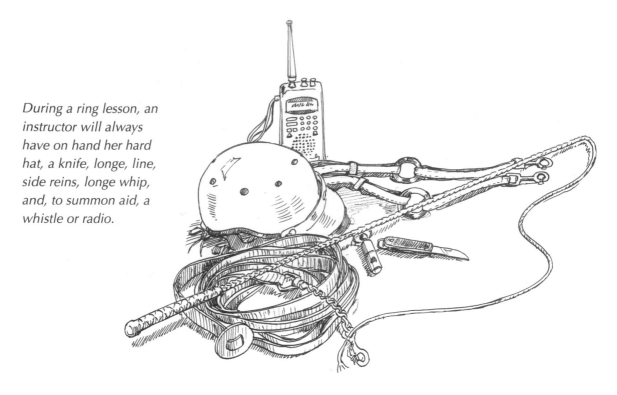

During a ring lesson, an instructor will always have on hand her hard hat, a knife, longe, line, side reins, longe whip, and, to summon aid, a whistle or radio.

Even though adult beginners may want only to take pleasant trail rides, they must understand the need to prepare for the unexpected.

Some adults will want to aim for competition or hardier riding, but remember, most have gained this desire by watching experienced riders who make it look easy. The adult needs to appreciate the importance of practice drills and the basics if the advanced skills are to be performed even passably well.

H. Sample Stable Guidelines for Riding Instructors

Most stable guidelines are just good common sense, but you only need one accident to find yourself in lawsuit territory. Know and follow these guidelines:

1. *Think first.* If you can imagine an accident arising out of a situation, then *don't get into that situation or quickly get control and get out of it.* This is serious lawsuit territory.
2. Instructors should not ask a student to perform a task that they themselves have not performed on the same school horse. The instructor should regularly ride school horses so that she will know them. This will keep them tuned up and will let the instructor know of potential problems. In the case of the instructor who is no longer physically able to ride, he should have observed the horse in the same situation with an assistant or another instructor.
3. If the weather is blustery, changeable, or recently cool, or if the horse wasn't turned out or wasn't ridden the day before, longe him. The rule is: "When in doubt, turn him out"; that is, longe him or ride him first yourself.
4. Dress properly in riding or neat casual clothes for the style you are teaching. Improper dress isn't likely to result in a lawsuit, but remember, jogging shorts

or sweats look unprofessional for the riding instructor. Some long cotton exercise leggings or riding sweats will work.

5. Always have with you during the lesson: your hard hat, a knife, longe line, side reins, longe whip, and, to summon aid, a whistle or radio. Also include a first-aid kit if you will take the lesson away from the barn. You may want a gun and a tranquilizer, but you can't have them.

6. You may take water with you to the ring or on the trail (and you **should** if it's hot). Leave the sodas at the barn and *don't even think about alcoholic beverages*. (No kidding; we see that more often than you would think.)

7. You know the safe and unsafe places to ride; don't ride in the unsafe places. Don't allow anyone else to ride there, either.

8. Never leave any students alone in the barn with a horse. They should not be permitted to go into any stalls, corrals, or pastures to catch or turn out a horse without supervision. Nor should they be permitted in any areas with loose horses.

9. **Hard hats are required at all times while mounted** (that's everybody, you too!) and while working around the horses. Consider horse areas "hard-hat areas." The first thing your students should do is put on their hard hats.

10. Watch the kids when they clean hooves; they tend to put their own feet where the horse will put his.

11. Check all tack or have one of the working students check it. The chief instructor should make the last check herself.

12. Students will **lead** horses to and from the arenas.

13. No one rides in the arenas without closing the gates. The instructor trying out a school horse or preparing for a show is the only exception to this rule. At shows, particularly dressage shows, the gates may be either open or absent. If this is going to cause a problem, the instructor will want to find out at home while she is riding alone in the arena. Under no circumstances should the instructor ride with the gate open while anyone else is present in the arena.

14. Riders will remain in line and motionless until all other riders are mounted and the girths or cinches are checked again. The last girth/cinch check before mounting should be made by the chief instructor of the lesson. We at the AAHS have found that some synthetic saddles tend to compress and that the girths or cinches need retightening immediately after mounting.

These items are no-no's!

You may bring water along, but leave sodas back at the barn.

Instructors should check all girths (including those on synthetic saddles) again 10 to 15 minutes into the lesson. After the warm-up is a good time. On the trail, check cinches after the ride has started. Do this separately for each student, even if the horse just came in from another lesson or ride.

15. Whenever the instructor gets equipment out, she must put it back. This includes poles and Bloks or standards in an arena. All empty jump cups should be removed to a bucket when not in use, not left on standards or on the ground.

16. When a student falls off, which will happen, make a written report and file it in the office. The report must include these details: who fell, from which horse, under what circumstances, who saw the incident, what the activity was, the weather, and anything else that seems pertinent.

    Naturally, if the fall is more than a bump or needs more than a Band-Aid, follow the "Emergency Procedures for People" first as outlined in Chapter 5, then make a formal accident report. In a serious accident, get statements from all observers. *The head instructor and owner or manager will want to know every time anybody comes off, skins a knee — anything.*

17. All students will remove saddle marks, put up grooming tools, rinse bits and girths, and put horses and tack in their proper places before they leave the stable area.

18. Do not tie horses hard and fast on the wash rack — wrap the rope around the hitch rail. At AAHS headquarters, we do not use cross ties.

19. No students will be transported in stable vehicles unless everybody is seat-belted in. Riding in the back of a truck is permitted only across the pasture, never on the road, and only when the truck can move at a very slow speed to ensure that riders don't get bounced out. Everyone in back must be sitting all the way back down on the floor of the bed.

20. It is the instructor's responsibility to spot tack and equipment that needs repair. Bring it to the office so that it can be fixed.

21. Read rule number one again.

I. Class Management

Effective class control makes learning easier. The instructor must at all times maintain frequent eye and voice contact with all students. Because of the movement of horses and wind conditions, this is very difficult if the class or the arena is large. Following are a few suggestions:

1. An effective class size is normally from four to six students per instructor. Keep the students within the range of your voice. Also it is easier to remember only four to six names at a time if you are teaching many classes. Remembering names can be an important safety measure, especially if it means getting a student's attention quickly to prevent her from making a mistake that could cause an accident.

2. When an instructor is working in a ring with the help of an assistant, the group size may be increased to 12 students, provided that the ring is large enough to allow safe spacing of about one horse's length or more between

riders with one-quarter of the rail left over. Each rider should see the feet of the horse ahead between the ears of his own horse. If the student sees only hocks, it's a warning; if he sees only the tail, it's a problem.

The instructor should act in a professional manner and focus her entire attention on students. What mistakes can you find in this photo?

3. Classes should start and end on time. The instructor should always be on time — no visiting or phone calls during a lesson unless it is an emergency requiring the instructor's *immediate* attention. The instructor may not leave a class unattended, especially a class of beginners.

4. Minimize student-to-student discussion.

5. Make directions short and easy to understand.

6. Make sure your directions have been heard.

7. Position students in relation to instructors so that all students can see and hear, and all instructors can see and hear.

8. In ground-school classes and mounted classes that are at the halt, students should not face the sun or distracting influences; nor should the instructor.

9. When talking against the wind, the instructor should project his voice toward students. He should be "upwind" whenever possible so that the wind will carry his voice toward the students.

10. After he explains a skill, the instructor should give a definite command for an individual or the group to commence action.

11. While the group is in motion, transitions from one gait to another always should be prefaced with a **command of preparation,** followed by a **pause** of approximately five seconds to allow time for a rider to prepare her horse, and then the **command of execution:** "Prepare to trot" or "Get ready to trot." The students need warning and so do the horses. Advanced riders and showring riders automatically give the horse a half-halt or preparation signal prior to the request. Beginners must learn to do this. The "prepare to" instruction becomes the half-halt or check of the advanced rider.

12. On the trail, maintain single-file order with safe spacing. Use hand and arm signals. Instructors should be at the head and rear of the group.
The Order Groups Should Follow
    • Instructor on quiet horse
    • Least experienced rider
    • More experienced
    • Most experienced
    • Assistant instructor or trail guide or intern.
(No one should pass lead instructor or wrangler.)

13. When asking a question of a student, ask the question saying the student's name last; otherwise, only the student named will listen to the question.

14. The safety of the students must be the primary concern in all classes and individual lessons.

J. Lesson Objectives

The instructor's goal has four components.

1. Students are not unduly placed at risk. Riding is risky enough anyway.
2. Students learn something each time or reinforce or improve a previous skill.
3. Students enjoy the lesson experience — maybe not every minute, because work is hard, but overall they must have a positive feeling about the lesson.
4. The instructor must also feel a sense of accomplishment in each lesson.

If you achieve all four of these points, you will be an effective instructor.

K. Teaching an Effective Lesson

Each lesson will have several parts, at least in the instructor's mind. If you have to write this on a little card and refer to it to get it all organized, then do it. A hodge-podge of a lesson is worthless. Here's what you'll want to include in the lesson.

Goals or Objectives

The instructor must have in mind a goal for each student in each lesson. What is the student going to learn today, and what skills are necessary to reach the goal? Break the goal into the sub-skills needed to accomplish it. Do they fit in the allotted lesson time or must the goal be broken down into separate lessons?

Safety Checks

An instructor must check each horse, its tack, each student, the weather, and the surroundings regardless of the level at which he is teaching or the ability of advanced students, even if the same horse and same tack were just in the ring.

Safe Instructors Evaluate Themselves

Instructors will teach better lessons if they keep the following questions in mind for self-evaluation and use them in analyzing each lesson.

1. In the review, were there any areas of misunderstanding? Did I correct them?
2. Did I meet my objectives?
3. How effective were my teaching aids? Did demonstrations and examples clarify the points I was making?
4. How could they be more effective?
5. Was safety emphasized? Did I relate everything I could to people on horse safety?
6. Was there ample time for practice? Did everybody finally get it? Can today's skill be next week's review?
7. Was there a good student response? If the response was poor, was it due to lack of enthusiasm on my part or a failure to make the lesson interesting or challenging? Do the students need more incentive to encourage a response?

8. Could all students see and hear the demonstrations? How many times was I asked to speak up? Did any student seem to ignore me?
9. How well did the horses respond to the student's directions? Do I have any school horses that need R & R or perhaps a change of work for a while? (This is particularly important with beginner horses or longe horses. Sometimes beginner schoolmaster horses can use some advanced riding or a good gallop cross-country to refresh them.)
10. Did I maintain a pleasant attitude? If not, why not?
11. Did I remember to summarize? Did I summarize effectively?
12. How could I have made the lesson better? How can I improve my lesson overall?

If the instructor checks this list after every lesson — it takes only a few minutes — the lessons will get better and better almost by themselves.

Chapter 4 — Review Questions

1. What are the criteria for not accepting a student? (page 35)

2. What are three student traits that hinder learning? (page 36)

3. What are four instructor factors that hinder learning? (page 36)

4. What should the instructor do when a rider falls during class? (page 40)

5. Whose responsibility is it to spot tack and equipment that needs repair? (page 40)

6. What is the recommended number of students in a class? (page 40)

7. Why is the "prepare to" command important? (page 41)

8. On the trail, what is the order of instructors and students in terms of experience? (page 41)

9. What must the instructor check before each lesson? (page 42)

10. What are five questions that should be a part of each instructor's self-evaluation? (page 42)

EMERGENCY AND STABLE PROCEDURES

One of the more frustrating aspects of teaching riding instruction has been to convey to instructors just how important it is to be prepared for emergencies. Too often, instructors don't want to believe an accident can occur in their class, and they tend to gloss over the material. But accidents do happen and probably will happen at some point. Certainly, preventing accidents is imperative, but so is being prepared to handle them.

Proper handling of an emergency can be crucial in minimizing the extent of injury — to both people and horses. It can also reduce the likelihood that you will be sued. If you are ever sued, proper handling of an emergency will help you defend yourself. Please read this material carefully.

A. Emergency Procedures for People

Post emergency phone numbers by each telephone. Have a written procedure for emergencies and provide it to each staff member. Staff should be trained and well rehearsed in the procedures. They should be reminded and drilled regularly so that no one can claim the staff was not trained. Each stable must have its own staff manual, and each staff member should have a copy of it. Appendix A contains an example of a staff manual.

Have a First-Aid Plan

Ask your private physician or Emergency Medical Service staff to help you establish your first-aid procedures and prepare first-aid kits for the barn and trail. Emergency supplies will vary in different localities and situations. It is wise to contact local medical personnel who can advise you on what is appropriate to have on hand, considering your horse-related activities.

The needs will be different depending on the climate and your particular activities, such as overnight camping, horse show trips, or mountainous area activities. Extreme heat or cold requires special attention. Emergency services also vary. Rural areas have different facilities from urban areas.

It is important to know which hospital serves your area and the average response time of your EMS. If you have no EMS in your area, it is imperative that you be trained in the best form of response. Your own physician will tell you. In this case, special first-aid training should be required. The AAHS requires current CPR and first-aid certification for all the instructors it certifies.

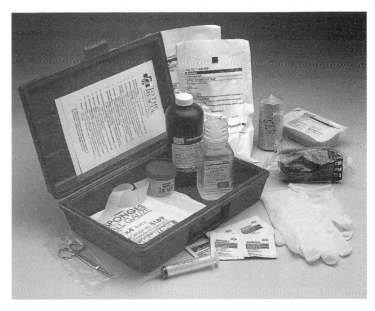

Have a physician or your local EMS staff help you establish a first-aid kit that's appropriate for your barn.

Always have all medical "consent to treatment" forms for all riders under 18 years of age in one binder that all staff members can find quickly and that can be taken to the doctor or hospital, or sent with the EMS vehicle. The hospital needs the originals, not copies. It is far better to have these forms and not need them than to need them and not have them. A minor might be refused treatment without them unless a parent or guardian is present. (See Appendix A for more on release forms.)

It is important that all instructors be certified in first aid and CPR. These courses are available from a variety of sources. The American Red Cross offers them at many locations; call your local Red Cross office to find the location of a course near your facility. These certifications must be renewed every few years, so keep them current.

Emergencies in the Ring

The following are procedures that have been used at AAHS headquarters. They may suit your individual situation. Again, check with your physician. *Unless the student is in danger of choking, never remove the helmet for her.*

1. If a student falls from a horse, halt the class calmly. The head instructor goes to the aid of the fallen rider and asks if the victim is all right. The assistant instructor reassures the class and positions them well apart to prevent further accidents.
2. The head instructor uses her first-aid training. She quickly assesses the extent of injury and responds accordingly.
3. If the rider lost his balance and slid off, the instructor may suggest, "Many riders take a fall now and then — it's all a part of learning, like your first bike ride or your first try at in-line skating. If you feel ready to remount, we'll see how you can improve your balance."

Instructors should remember that most falls are caused by loss of balance and are not serious. Sometimes, though, the rider loses his wind and is truly frightened. Reassurance is the best attitude to maintain. However, the rider should get up by himself, because this independent action usually will indicate that there is no serious injury.

4. If the rider refuses to remount, he should not be bullied or belittled. Restore his confidence by encouraging him to handle the horse from the ground (grooming, leading) until he is ready to remount. He may not remount the same day. Don't make it into a big deal.

5. In case of injury, do not move the student who does not get up himself. Stay with him. Blow the whistle you always carry for help or send your assistant for help. Try to determine the nature and extent of the injury. Remember your first-aid training.

   An assistant should either take the others back to the barn or have them dismount and remain unmounted, holding their horses, while the head instructor attends to the injured rider. Calmness and reassurance are important.

6. If medical treatment is indicated, take the injured person to the hospital, if he can move on his own. If he cannot move or should not be moved, call 911.

7. If the injured person is under the age of 18, send for the binder containing the medical consent forms, which should have been signed by parents and notarized. Take the binder with you when you take him to the hospital, clinic, or doctor, or send him off in an ambulance — otherwise he may be refused treatment unless his life is threatened. (A sample release form is included in Appendix A.)

8. If you take or accompany the injured person to the hospital, be sure that someone will put up all horses and that all students are accounted for.

9. If someone else accompanies the injured person, briefly explain what has happened in a matter-of-fact way and continue the lesson in a low-key manner.

10. Show concern; state facts clearly; do not ever talk in terms of fault. Say, "Mary fell off and sprained her wrist," not, "Oh, if I had only longed Fantasy first, Mary wouldn't have fallen." You don't know that to be a fact, so don't say it.

11. Fill out an accident report and notify the owner, manager, or head instructor or trainer.

12. Call the victim and/or victim's parents to show continuing concern. You must care. They must know you care.

13. Interview all witnesses before the story gets blown out of proportion, and a simple tumble becomes a wild buck.

14. **Stay calm. Do not panic, do not panic, do not panic.**

Emergencies on the Trail

Riding way from the barn requires some special emergency preparation.

1. If a student falls from his horse, the instructor or wrangler at the lead asks the riders to halt. In a **calm and reassuring tone,** she *tells riders to dismount* and to lead their horses well apart from each other.

2. The head instructor quickly ties her horse by the halter (AAHS recommends that a horse on a trail ride wear his halter under the bridle with the lead line tied cavalry-style around his neck) to a tree or solid post; if in an open field, she should move her horse well away from others or hand the reins to the assistant or a competent rider.

3. Quickly and quietly assess the extent of injury and respond accordingly. The instructor's fanny pack should contain necessary first-aid materials. Ask your physician's advice for setting this up, along with the other first-aid kits for people.

4. If the injury requires an emergency vehicle, an assistant instructor should radio, phone, or return to the barn to summon aid. The head instructor must remain with the injured person and maintain control of the class. Do not permit students to become alarmed or hysterical. That could cause a second accident.

    Control the conversation by directing it away from the immediate problem. Talk about something else. Sometimes, riders will talk about the situation anyway, so it may be a good opportunity for the instructor to explain the horse's action while at the same time maintaining control of the class. **Never, ever, discuss fault.**

5. If the rider is not injured but refuses to remount, the head instructor may lead the group while the assistant walks with the student and attempts to encourage him to remount.

We advise that on the trail, horses wear their halters under their bridles with lead ropes tied cavalry-style around their necks or carried separately by an instructor or guide. Follow these 7 steps to tie a rope cavalry-style.

All photos by Dick Pond

Generally, after the fear has subsided and wounded pride has healed a bit, the rider will remount his or another horse in which he has more confidence.

6. In case of a runaway horse, tell the class to halt, dismount, and hold their horses. The head instructor should follow, but not chase, the runaway horse and attempt to talk the rider through the problem: the emergency stop, doubling, or circling. Most horses will stay near the group. The emergency dismount may be necessary, but only as a last resort. This command may be given at the discretion of the instructor.

B. Preventing and Handling Emergencies in Horses

We've used the routine at AAHS headquarters as an example of safe stable management. We recommend that stable duties be learned and performed in the same order each day to lessen the chance of mistakes and mishaps.

Provide feed three times a day to horses not turned out in *good* pasture. Offer hay first, then water, then grain, to discourage gobbling. Always feed horses in the same order and at the same time so they know when to expect to be fed. Horses like to look forward to something and then see it happen when expected.

Feed rations should be posted in the feed room if rations are mixed individually, or on stall doors if feeding from a cart. As much as possible, the same people should mix and feed. Weigh all feed or mark weights on containers, such as coffee cans.

For horses that are fed three times a day, we use a basic ration of 6 to 10 pounds of high-quality feed and 15 to 20 pounds of hay per horse per day. We give supplements during the morning feed whenever possible for horses who need them. If the grass is good, the horses stay out through the noon feeding, so only horses confined at midday or those with special nutritional needs receive lunch. It is important to emphasize that a mistake in feeding — even a small one — can cripple or cause the death of a horse.

Stalls should be cleaned well daily. We recommend at least six to eight inches of shavings or other bedding. After the removal of manure and urine-soaked bedding, we advise turning all bedding over, bottom to top, to aerate the floor and kill ammonia-forming, anaerobic bacteria. We don't "bank" stalls unless they are larger than 12 feet by 12 feet.

We prefer buckets to automatic waterers, so we can see how much each horse is drinking. The buckets should be cleaned thoroughly and disinfected with diluted chlorine bleach at least once a week. They should be cleaned more frequently if necessary or if a different horse is to use that stall. We hang buckets away from feed and hay so that neither messes up the water. Check for bucket poopers — some horses do this.

Corrals, loafing pens, and paddocks need a weekly cleaning, more often if necessary. Because it's a valuable fertilizer, contain manure and spread it in a fashion that best preserves it as a soil nutrient and prevents pollution of water sources. Pastures should be harrowed to break up manure — horses won't graze where they poop. Harrowing pastures to spread manure also allows the sun to kill parasite and fly larvae and eggs.

Horses need to be handled daily, but they also need to be turned out, if not in a pasture, at least in a paddock for a minimum of two hours per day. If that isn't possible, allow the horse some freedom, such as a trail ride under saddle after his workout, and try to hand graze him at least 30 minutes each day.

While the horse needs freedom, he also needs human handling on a daily basis. This is your opportunity to check him thoroughly and also prevents the horse from giving in to his tendency to revert to any prior unpleasant behavior. Daily handling also reinforces the horse's association with humans with pleasurable activities, such as feeding and grooming.

Ideally, the horse would be confined in a stall or corral at night, then caught, led, and turned out each morning. Reverse this process in the evening. Thus, the horse is handled by a human and thoroughly checked twice each day. You may leave horses out at night with proper fencing, away from roads and with adequate water and shelter.

After each feeding, mix up the next unless feeding from a cart. No unauthorized personnel, such as students or customers, should be allowed in feed rooms or to mix feed. The manager or designated person should keep track of feed and hay and try to manage feed orders and other supplies on a regular basis. The turnout schedule should be posted and kept up to date.

Margaret Thomas

Stalls should be well cleaned daily.

Emergency Procedures for Horses

The best person to set up the first-aid and emergency procedures for your barn is your own veterinarian. Then you always will use a procedure that he is comfortable with, and that is compatible with his treatment philosophy. When calling the veterinarian, it is important to provide specific details. If you suspect illness, be ready when you make that first call to give the veterinarian the horse's vital signs, as well as symptoms.

Normal Vital Signs
- Temperature (99–101°F)
- Pulse (32– 44 beats per minute, higher in foals)
- Respiration (8 –16 breaths per minute)
- Capillary refill (push test on gums, 1–2 seconds)
- Test for dehydration (pinch test on neck, 1–2 seconds)

Your veterinarian can help you learn to recognize healthy and unhealthy gut sounds and to recognize not only which leg the lame horse is favoring, but also where on the leg the pain is, such as above the knee, below the knee, or in the foot.

Emergency First Aid for Horses
When in doubt, call the veterinarian!

Our veterinarian provided these instructions. We offer them only as an example. They are not universal and may be contrary to your veterinarian's treatment philosophy. Develop your procedures with your own veterinarian.

If the horse is insured, the veterinarian must give all medications or give you written instructions to do so. If an ill horse is insured, you must notify the insurance company and have its permission to destroy the horse if an illness or injury progresses to this unfortunate stage of severity. In most cases, the insurance company will want a postmortem examination performed. Tell your veterinarian that the horse is insured as soon as you acquire the insurance and each time you call the veterinarian regarding illness of an insured horse.

1. **Suspected Colic.** Colic is pain that can be caused by a variety of problems ranging from a simple case of gas to a life-threatening torsion, or twisting, of the intestines. It is the number one killer of horses. Learn about it.

   A horse with colic will be restless, and may bite or toss the head toward the flanks, roll or get up and down. There may be minimal gut sounds. Some horses with colic twitch or raise their upper lip, circle, paw, or go off feed. Many veterinarians will advise that you keep an injectable medication on hand to control colic pain until they can arrive. Follow their directions. If the horse is insured, notify the insurance company.

   If You Suspect Colic
   - Call the veterinarian and be prepared immediately with vital signs. Don't wait around to see if the horse's symptoms let up. Early medical treatment can in some cases prevent a simple case of colic from progressing to one that requires far more extensive intervention. Some causes of colic require surgery, and in these cases, you'll want to get the horse to a surgical facility as soon as possible.
   - Call the owner, if appropriate. Give the facts. Say the veterinarian is on the way. Don't exaggerate or panic.
   - Keep the horse from rolling, which may make matters worse. Walk the horse if necessary to keep him from rolling.
   - Slight symptoms can precede a major colic episode of surgical proportions; violent symptoms can precede the mildest gas colic. The difference is in the individual with the symptoms. With colic, minimal symptoms do not necessarily mean minimal danger. Remember, colic is the number one killer of horses.

2. **Suspected Founder** (acute laminitis). This is intense inflammation in the foot or feet and can be very serious. Horses with this condition may walk as if on eggs or may walk with heels down first to stay off the toes. Usually, only the front feet are affected, and to keep weight off the painful feet, the horse will rock back on his hind feet and draw them up under him. If the back hooves are affected, the horse may rock forward; if all four feet are involved, he may look as though he's trying to bring all four feet under him. His hooves may be hot, and he may refuse to move at all.

Call the veterinarian immediately if you suspect founder or laminitis. Have ready the horse's vital signs and specifics on heat in hooves.

3. **Lameness.** This is a sign that the horse has a pain, often in the foot or leg. Unless lameness is due to something obvious that can be readily corrected and that resolves the lameness, such as a stick caught in the shoe, it's best to call your veterinarian. Be sure to tell the veterinarian which foot or leg is affected, and if there is any heat or swelling.

4. **Deep Laceration.** This is a deep tear in the skin. Clean it first with cold water. Gently scrub out dirt. If necessary, apply pressure bandage to stop bleeding. Call your veterinarian with exact details. You may be instructed to bring the horse in or the veterinarian may come to the stable. Do not administer treatment without instruction; some formerly accepted practices have fallen into serious disfavor, such as cleaning a fresh wound with hydrogen peroxide, which can damage tissue.

5. **Puncture Wound.** This is a wound that penetrates the skin and underlying tissues while leaving only a small opening on the surface. A surface scrub will not clean a puncture wound.

    Irrigate with sterile saline solution, apply a pressure bandage, and call the veterinarian with details.

6. **Object Stuck in the Flesh.** If it can be easily extracted, such as a small sliver of wood or a piece of wire, do so and treat as a puncture wound. If it is a big thing, don't pull it out — call the veterinarian.

7. **Object in the hoof.** If it can be extracted, do so. Call the veterinarian with details and soak the hoof twice daily with all the Epsom salts you can dissolve in the hottest water that you can tolerate with your bare hand.

8. **Eyes.** Do not use a steroid preparation on an eye unless the veterinarian has seen the eye and advises you to do so. A misapplication could cause permanent blindness.

    Wash with a sterile saline solution. In cases of wounds and sickness, let the veterinarian decide which, if any, antibiotic is appropriate. Do not extract an object stuck in the eye yourself, although it may wash out with the sterile saline solution.

1. In what two areas should all instructors be certified? (page 45)

2. What should the instructors do when a rider falls during a class in the ring? (pages 45-46)

3. True or False: In case of injury, do not move the student who does not get up himself. (page 46)

4. How many times a day should you provide feed to horses not turned out in pasture? (page 48)

5. In what order do you give grain, hay, and water and why might the order matter? (page 48)

6. Why is a water bucket in a stall a better choice than an automatic waterer? (page 48)

7. Who should advise you on the establishment of emergency procedures for the horses in your barn? Explain. (page 49)

8. What is a horse's normal temperature? Normal respiratory rate? Normal capillary refill time? (page 49)

9. What is the number one killer of horses? (page 50)

10. What are five signs of possible colic? (page 50)

AAHS–Certified Instructor Guidelines

In this chapter, we will learn more about the particulars that qualify an instructor for AAHS certification.

A. Who Is the Safe Instructor?

A safe instructor is one who:
- Is at least 21 years of age for full AAHS certification as Safety-Certified Riding Instructor and Instructor/Trainer; shows maturity.
- Has at least a high school diploma.
- Is an experienced rider, with at least five years of serious, regular experience, preferably as a professional.
- Has had some formal riding education.
- Participates in shows or events, such as team penning, polo, or games.
- Exhibits a high level of interest and a desire to improve.
- Has ridden many horses in many settings.
- Can recognize whether a horse is suitable for a particular rider.
- Has good rapport with horses and understands them.

B. The Instructor Knows and Understands

The instructor should recognize a safe horse and safe horse/rider combination. Beginners should be on sound, older, gentle horses with solid training. Timid students need solid horses. There is much that cannot be controlled in riding instruction, but with beginners, we must control whatever we can, because these students can control almost nothing.

We must not only give them gentle horses of calm temperament; tack and equipment must be in good condition, properly fitted, and adjusted; and the facilities must be safe. There must be quality instruction as well.

Even the sweetest horse is unpredictable and can buck, shy, stop, bite, kick, squeeze you against a wall or fence, or run back to the barn. All horses are good some of the time; some horses are good most of the time; some horses are bad most of the time; all horses are bad some of the time. Stick with the ones who are good most of the time. Avoid those with dangerous histories.

Once a horse does something bad — even if the action was caused by an insensitive student or instructor error — you cannot afford to keep that horse on your school or trail string. If he did it once, he could do it again. The second time is foreseeable — foreseeable usually means "suable."

It is extremely important to match your horses and students thoughtfully and to supervise them carefully, or you will end up losing a valuable school horse. A school horse may make one mistake; he may not make two.

A horse's bad behavior can be caused by discomfort, such as soreness, a bellyache, the rider's use of the aids, or overtaxing by the instructor. An uncomfortable horse can and probably will cause an accident eventually.

A safe instructor will spot the problem horse and rider pair by automatically using a mental checklist.

How does the horse appear overall?
- Ears moving or flat back?
- Eyes calm or excited?
- Gaits normal or off?
- Stands quietly or fidgets?
- Tail quiet?
- Equipment fits properly — cinch/girth tightened three times, bridle correctly adjusted?

How does the rider appear?
- Stiff and forward? (which can irritate a horse)
- Well seated but tense, probably squeezing with legs?
- Reins too tight — legs too tight?
- Rider off balance — horse veers one way or other?
- Rider preoccupied, not paying attention?
- Does the rider appear comfortable?

How do the pair appear?
- Are they standing or moving quietly?
- Do they seem uncomfortable and agitated?

If the horse is not standing quietly, get the rider off immediately, check the tack, and possibly longe or ride the horse yourself. If horse does not calm down, put the student on another horse. An agitated horse is a warning signal. Once you've had your warning, the accident is foreseeable, and you must avoid that situation or be prepared to pay ($$$) the consequences.

If the horse becomes agitated when moving under saddle, check the rider's position, use of aids, and the fit and adjustment of tack. If nothing wrong can be found even after the instructor rides the horse, the horse must not be used in the lesson and should be examined more carefully, later, perhaps by the veterinarian.

The pair must start off comfortable and relaxed, and they must finish the lesson comfortable and relaxed. Horse and rider must be at ease in order to learn and to avoid injuries.

Common Dangerous Actions
- Leading from the right (wrong) side
- Standing in front of or directly behind a horse
- Dragging the end of the lead rope or bridle reins
- Putting an arm through loops of rope, reins, or longe line
- Looping rope or reins around the hand
- Not taking reins over the horse's head when leading a bridled horse
- Standing in front of horse's front feet while turning the horse
- Yelling or screaming around horses
- Running around horses
- Stepping under the lead rope of a tied horse
- Touching a horse's head without the horse's permission
- Walking behind someone else's horse within the "kicking range"

The dangers inherent in these actions were explained and discussed during the initial safety lecture on the nature of the horse. A safe instructor frequently reminds students to avoid these behaviors so she doesn't have to race to get them out of harm's way and maybe doesn't make it.

C. Preparing for the Safe Mounted Lesson

Remember, your first lesson with any student was the safety lecture.
Before students arrive for mounted lessons, the instructor should:
1. Evaluate the weather — can we ride?
2. Check the horses to be used — they should appear contented and alert, with no signs of discomfort.
3. Check equipment to be used, even though students will do a safety check as well.
4. Check the facility — the riding surface is okay; obstacles are removed, there are no empty jump cups, and nothing is hanging on standards or the arena fence.
5. Look at the last lesson plan (you did have a plan?) — were there problems that need to be worked on (near accident, perhaps)? Review and/or adjust the lesson plan for the upcoming class, treating each student as an individual and

Confiscate the gum!

as a member of the class. Each lesson should build on the previous lesson and attempt to solve previous problems.

6. Match horses and students and tack.

When students arrive, the instructor should:
1. Evaluate the students — are they relaxed and eager?
2. Check equipment and attire. Students should have on an approved helmet, which will have a label in it that reads ASTM/SEI–approved. Students also should be wearing long pants, and boots with one-inch heels. No baggy pants or oversized T-shirts, or shirttails hanging out to catch on things.

   Also, supervise the tacking-up area. A safe saddling area is one to which horses can be brought and then tied safely, not so close together as to be able to kick another horse, and away from traffic. It is an area designed for that purpose alone. Crowding is dangerous. The instructor should be able to see all students at all times. If more than one student needs personal attention, have an assistant or advanced student give help. Help must be readily available.

3. Horses are led to the riding area with an assistant present, and gate is closed.
4. Line up, then check girths and equipment again.
5. "Prepare to mount" — mount students, one at a time for beginners, and have them remain standing. Horses are not allowed to move off immediately. More experienced riders may be given the instruction, "Class, mount up." Check girths again once riders are mounted, and one more time 10 to 15 minutes after mounting. Many horses "bloat up" and let that air out after the rider is seated. And remember, we've found that some synthetic saddles compress under the weight of the rider, loosening the cinch or girth. Safe instructors won't let saddles slip!

D. The Mounted Part of the Lesson

Once the students are mounted, have them move off and then proceed as follows:
1. "Prepare to walk forward and track left." Then say "Class, walk forward." They should ride straight to the rail as a group, side by side, then all turn left. The safe instructor or guide (if this is pre–trail ride instruction) should then carefully observe the attitudes of the students now mounted, and the horses, now moving. If all seems well, continue. **Never leave one horse isolated in the arena or on the trail.** *Lesson horses and trail horses* especially don't like to be left alone. Leaving them alone is a common error.
2. At the beginning of each ride, the safe instructor will review safety procedures and the accidents that can result from ignoring those procedures.
   • **Maintain correct spacing** — one to two horse lengths between horses: each student should see the two hind feet of the horse ahead between the ears of his own mount and no farther back and no closer — seeing the hocks is a warning; seeing the tail, she's in trouble. Correct spacing prevents:

a. The horse behind getting kicked
   b. Spooking the horse in front
   c. The horse in back speeding up suddenly
   d. A runaway ride
- **All riders halt:**
   a. When a student's horse goes too fast
   b. When a rider or horse falls — instructor may ask all riders to dismount
   c. When any situation occurs requiring a class of beginners to reposition — that is to correct spacing
   d. When someone must dismount, remount, or falls
   e. When students or customers tell the instructor they dropped something
   f. When tack must be repaired or tack is broken

Each instructor will want to enlarge this list depending on the individual situation.

3. Safe instructor's suggested *management* and *control* of a mounted ride in the arena:

- Demonstrate three halts of progressive severity.
- In an early lesson, teach the stages of the emergency stop. Students are more confident when they know that they can gain control.
- Students at a walk may perform school figures (circles, figure 8, change of rein through the circle, half turns) as a group or individually. All students should know the school figures so that the instructor can easily move the class around the arena. Walking exercises should take 5 to 10 minutes. Students should use the time to do their own stretching exercises if this can be done safely.
- Some students may be able to trot on rail and do figures. If there are any doubts or if any problems show up, have the students work in small groups or individually at the walk, using your assistant(s), until they are ready to trot. If you do not have enough assistants, you must divide the class.

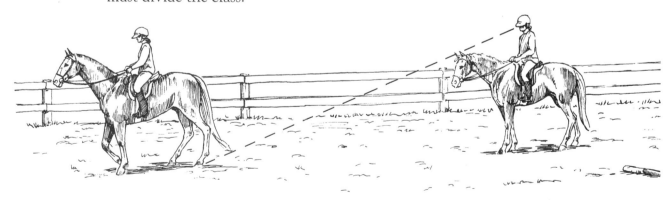

Maintain proper spacing. Remember, seeing the hooves between the ears is good; hocks between ears is a warning; a tail means you are in trouble.

- A student whose position deteriorates or whose horse speeds up repeatedly **must** be considered to be at risk and must be dealt with individually and with slower work.

4. Beginning faster work: Horses used must be consistent, fairly smooth, and should be voice-trained to "Whoa," *dependably*, whenever asked.

    While it is usually best to begin canter work on a longe line, that is not always possible. Only the most experienced instructors should attemp to longe riders. They need much experience longeing and also must have a suitable, experienced longe horse. (See Chapter 11 for more on longeing.) Having the student experience the movement of the canter while the instructor maintains control of the horse at a steady pace is valuable. Horses often volunteer to canter after cavalletti and a cross pole. Cantering becomes natural and simple. Remember that:

    - No canter work should begin before the student has mastered the trot or jog, both sitting and rising, and the light seat or two-point position to ensure the student's security and the horse's comfort.
    - The safe instructor will discuss in depth the basic aids for the canter or lope and will demonstrate a few strides of each. The goal at this point is to teach the student what the gait feels like and how to sit it.
    - Each student, one at a time, is asked to try the new gait, proceeding around the rail of a small ring to the end of the line or to the instructor. A few strides is sufficient for the first time. This is not the time to worry about leads.
    - Another student should join the last horse if crossing a ring so that no horse is isolated. However, working from the front of the class around to the end of the line is better.

When introducing the canter or lope, have each student try the new gait one at a time. (This student should have her leg back a bit more for perfect alignment.)

5. The safe instructor's management of the lesson outside the arena: Whenever possible, all rides begin and end in an enclosed, but not crowded, arena. Riders must be able to spread out in a line to mount and dismount safely. The safe instructor remembers at all times that the purpose of a lesson on the trail is not only to give student and horse a break from the ring or arena, but also to teach the student how to ride safely out in the open away from the stable area.

    The student must be taught "rules of the road" — traffic law as it pertains to horses. These may vary from state to state. However, avoid riding on or by roads as much as possible.

    All students should be familiar with hand signals for *stop*, *left*, and *right*.

Each person seeing a hazard should call it out ("Hole" or "Beware hole") clearly and point to its location; others should "pass it on."

- **In the meadow or on the trail:**
  a. Riders usually should be single file at the walk in the following order:
     1. lead guide or instructor on quietest horse (the lead horse is the one most likely to spook)
     2. least proficient rider
     3. more proficient rider
     4. most proficient rider
     5. drag guide or assistant instructor
  b. A 4:1 ratio of riders to instructor is preferred, 6:1 is allowed, with a maximum of 12 riders and two staff in any one ride. Three staff members are better, with one in the middle, as the drag rider cannot see well more than six riders ahead. We prefer one staff member for every six riders.
  c. There *always* must be two staff if you cannot communicate with the barn by sight or sound, that is, if you are out of sight and have no radio or other signaling device.
  d. The safe instructor will not take a ride in the meadow unless all members of the ride have previously demonstrated proficiency at the trot and know how *not* to canter.
  e. An unmannerly horse or disobedient student is a risk to all and should not be allowed.
  f. The safe instructor, after surveying the terrain, weather, horses, and riders' attitudes, again may allow trotting by individuals in such a manner that those trotting are trotting around the other riders to prevent halted horses from feeling abandoned. Riders might also trot in pairs around several individual riders serving as markers.
  g. As a general rule, a safe instructor *never* allows cantering in the field. The exception is with advanced, highly capable students; they may canter one at a time. Never canter as a group, as the horses will begin to frolic with each other. These are class lessons on stable-owned horses — you cannot afford a wreck!

- **Far out on the trail, in the forest with lions, tigers, and bears:**
  a. Horses should wear halters with lead ropes under their bridles.

When on the trail, push branches away from your body, then let them go by. Don't try to hold a branch for the next rider.

Lead ropes should be tied around the horse's neck with a cavalry knot, or tied separately and unattached to the halter.

b. As in the ring class, the safe instructor begins all rides in an enclosed area whenever possible and will not take riders on trail who are not proficient at the trot.

c. The same ratio of instructors to students or customers and the same lineup as described above should be used. There must be one staff for each six riders and no fewer than two staff *ever*. There should be three staff with 12 riders so that every seventh person is a staff member.

d. The safe instructor maintains a single-file line with one horse's length between each horse — no exceptions. Here also, each rider should see the feet of the horse ahead between the ears of his own mount.

e. Passing another horse is not permitted.

f. The safe instructor ensures that all horses are only walking, especially up and down hills; a suddenly trotting horse can cause a pileup, or a runaway horse, or a runaway ride.

g. The safe instructor is constantly reminding students of the trail do's and don'ts and why we have them:

DO'S	DON'TS
Do push protruding branches up and over your own head.	**Don't** hold a branch so that it slaps the next rider.
Do use your hand to push away from a tree that might catch your knee.	**Don't** let a tree catch your kneecap. Push yourself away with your hand.
Do cross roads all at once. If asked to dismount by the instructor, do remount on uphill side of the horse or maneuver the horse into a low place on the trail.	**Don't** cross a road one at a time in a line, unless flag persons can safely stop traffic. The flag persons should not be the lead or drag riders.
Do remount on the uphill side.	**Don't** remount on the downhill side of a horse. The stirrup is harder to reach, and you could pull the horse off balance and on top of you.
Do tie horses with halters and leads.	**Don't** tie horses by the reins or leave them to drag.
Do ride with at least two people (three is better) — preferably experienced — one to render first aid, the other to go for help.	**Don't** ride out with only one instructor. If you have an accident and CPR is required, who will get help?
Do keep a staff member in the front of the line at all times.	**Don't** allow anyone to pass lead staff member.

Chapter 6 — Review Questions

1. Beginners need _____ horses with _____ temperaments. (page 54)

2. How can matching the wrong student with a school horse end up causing the loss of a good horse in a school string? (page 54)

3. Describe the instructor's preparation for the safe mounted lesson. (pages 55-56)

4. What is meant by "correct spacing" and why is it important? (pages 56-57)

5. Which students may go on a trail ride? Who may trot and when? Who may canter and when? (pages 58-59)

6. Which horse in a trail-ride line is most likely to be startled, and who should be riding it? (page 59)

7. Why is it better to have three staff instead of two on a trail ride with 12 students? (page 59)

8. What is the correct spacing on the trail? Explain. (page 60)

9. What are four "do's" for trail riding? (page 60)

10. What are four "don'ts" for trail riding? (page 60)

CONSTRUCTING A LESSON PLAN

Experienced instructors never walk into the ring without a plan. If they have new students, they use warm-up time to evaluate riders and devise a plan.

A. Why a Plan Is Important

The instructor needs a plan in order to reach the goal. Each lesson must have a goal. Students must understand the goal. The goal must be attainable with some effort by the average student during the lesson. Its attainment must be measurable by the instructor. Some students may go on beyond that lesson's goal, but each must achieve something.

The lesson parts must all fit into the allotted time, usually one hour. There are five elements to a lesson:

1. **Introduction:** your name, their names, or a greeting if you know each other or a bit of chitchat; what is planned for the lesson, and why it's important.
2. **Review:** Go over what you did last time. Were there any problems? What happened in the last lesson, if it wasn't taught by you?
3. **Explanation/Demonstration:** statement and example of a goal that day; make it attainable. Demonstrate the goal.
4. **Practice:** The students attempt and repeat the skill.
5. **Summary:** The students explain the skill and how to perform it. Summary must agree with #3 or the lesson will have to be retaught next lesson.

A lesson plan is important because of what it teaches the instructor. It requires the instructor to think out each part of the lesson and to set specific goals in terms of skills the students must learn. That is a process that an instructor may tend to skip, unless the discipline of a lesson plan requires it.

While it may not be necessary for you as an instructor to write a lesson plan for each class or each lesson, it will be necessary to think through each phase of your instruction and to divide the skills into manageable, interrelated goals and parts or units.

Go for the Goal
- A good instructor always has a plan.
- The plan always has a goal.
- The goal is measurable by the instructor.
- The average student can reach the goal.

Teaching All the Components of a Skill

The way many instructors fail to reach their goal — and this is especially true of those instructors who also are good horse trainers — is by not teaching all the components of a particular skill because they are unaware of all the parts or subskills that make up that skill. They are not conscious of all they are doing when they ride. This is one reason why it is so important for an instructor to be able to perform *correctly* all the skills being taught. Only then can the instructor analyze the skill and break it down into its basic parts.

Each of the skills and subskills is a goal. It is a difference of perception only, but one that is critical to the student. That the instructor could perform the skill well at some time in the past is acceptable. The instructor must teach "feel," so she must know how each skill feels.

Breaking Skills Down into Parts

As you begin to teach, your students will tell you by their actions if you have adequately analyzed each skill or goal and broken it down into its appropriate parts. If you have, they can perform the skill. If you have left something out or made an error, they cannot. So listen to your students, watch them. **Remember,** the student will retain more if he understands why he is doing something — specify the mechanical, not philosophical, reason. He will also retain more if the skill is taught in steps that can be counted off.

Instructors Should Aim to:
- Teach the *"why"* of skills or goals.
- Teach the *steps* or subskills of the goals.
- *Condense* the steps to something easy — "1-2-3-4."

Keep These Points in Mind:
- Skill (a goal) to be taught — a description and its safety implications
- Subskills (parts or steps of a skill) — will it all fit in the allotted time?
- What has been learned — summary: skills, subskills, includes terminology
- Review Lesson A at the beginning of Lesson B

Remember, students take away only what the instructor puts in.

Before the instructor deals with correct alignment or position, she must be able to get the student on and off the horse safely. We could just give the student a leg up, but what would he learn? We have to back up and find a way to get the student mounted **safely, correctly,** and in a way that he will remember the next time.

Correctness is especially important because **mounting is the most dangerous skill a beginner will learn.** During mounting there is that moment when the student is half on and half off the horse and is extremely vulnerable.

Learning to mount a horse correctly and safely most definitely is a goal, but not necessarily mounting from the ground. Many beginners may not be able to mount unaided after the first mounting lesson or even after several lessons.

Mounting must be broken down into teachable — and achievable — components. These parts are the subskills for the lesson. Everyone will achieve some of them. Mounting safely and correctly remains the overall goal.

Goal: Mounting

Students not tall enough or limber enough may mount from a block. Remember, the overall goal is "mounting," not "mounting from the ground."

The Steps or Subskills

1. Take the reins in your left hand, short enough for control, but not tight. Check girth or cinch.
2. Grab the mane and reins at the same time in your left hand. Always hold the reins so that you always have some control.
3. Face the tail of the horse; you can more easily swing up if he moves off.
4. Take the stirrup with your right hand and turn it toward you.
5. Put your left toe in the left stirrup; if you put the right toe in the left stirrup, you will end up facing the tail!
6. Grab the pommel or cantle of the saddle with your right hand. Put your toe in the girth or cinch (not in the horse) or turn your foot parallel to the horse, toe forward.

   Do not grab both the front and the back of a saddle, as you can pull it off the horse or pull the horse off balance or on top of you. You will find it difficult to get an unbalanced horse to stand quietly as he will want to regain his balance — horses that expect to be pulled off balance will not

Maximize Student Learning Experiences

If it can be done safely, it can be better to let the student make a mistake so he'll remember. For example, let him try to mount by putting the right toe in the stirrup — he would end up facing the tail. But stop him before he gets all the way up.

want to stand to be mounted. Why? Because the horse wants to remain able to stand up.

7. Take three hops and spring up, swing your right leg over the horse, and put your right foot in the stirrup as you **ease** your seat gently into the saddle. *Caution:* Do not bump the rump of your horse with your leg. Do not flop into the saddle. Either action may startle your horse and leave you sitting in the dirt. Keep your upper body as close to the horse as possible to aid his balance.

    Caution the student to insist that the horse stand quietly during mounting and for a minute or so afterward. Otherwise, the horse will get into the habit of moving off right away and will not always stand quietly for mounting.

When the student understands the process and can mount either from the ground or from a mounting block, you can condense the subskills into a 1-2-3-4 count-off, and the student or the whole class can spring up on "4." Here's how the count-off goes:

1. *Check girth — don't leave out this step!*
   (If it is too loose, tighten it. Two fingers should fit under the cinch under the horse's belly.)
2. *Take the reins and mane in left hand.*
3. *Face the tail, turn the stirrup, and put your left toe in the stirrup and cinch or girth, but not in the horse's side.*
4. *Take three hops, spring up, swing your right leg over the rump, and sit gently down.*

Remember, "spring" up, not pull up. What subgoals can we expect the student to have achieved from learning the mounting steps? (This also lets you know if the lesson was understood.)

The Student:
- Has learned the 1-2-3-4 mounting method
- Has acquired the following vocabulary: *reins, mane, pommel, cantle, girth, rump, stirrup, seat*
- Can explain the following concepts: We face the tail so that if the horse does move off, we can more easily spring up; we must control the toe while mounting so we do not stick it into the horse which will cause him to move
- Understands why some horses fidget while being mounted
- Knows that the position half on/half off is precarious

When mounting, don't bump the rump.

- Knows always to check the girth or cinch one last time before mounting and how to check the girth
- Knows not to bump the horse's rear end with his own right leg

You probably can add to this list, but now you know that these are the subgoals of the lesson and also the **summary.** The student should be encouraged to respond, not only to help his memory, but also so you and he will know how much he has understood and is likely to retain. This is also the **review** in the next lesson.

The more times students have to recall information and respond, the better they will remember it. The more times they do it, the better they will do it — this is "practice."

If you think through each lesson, you will have your goals and know how to measure them. Soon you will do that by habit.

Goal: Dismounting

Use the same procedure, with an emphasized caution: **AAHS does not recommend a "step-down" dismount, ever. We do not have to be half on/half off to get off.**

Subskills for Method 1
1. Swing your right leg back over horse's rump
2. Lean over saddle on your tummy.
3. Kick off the left stirrup.
4. Slide down.

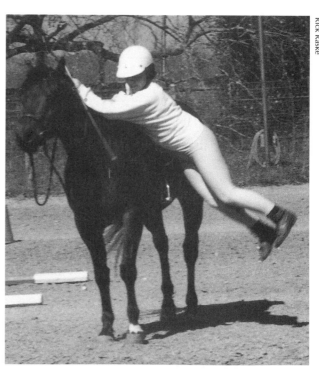

To dismount, take both feet out of stirrups, press on horse's neck, swing right leg over back, and slide down.

Subskills for Method 2 (This is better.)

1. Take your feet out of both stirrups.
2. Press down on the neck or pommel with your hands.
3. Swing your right leg over the back and slide down, all in one motion.

A major mounting/dismounting subskill is to be able to swing the right leg over the rump without bumping it.

When you are teaching any skill, you must analyze all of its parts and teach all the parts, even though you may abbreviate them later, for example turning seven steps into a 1-2-3-4 mounting method.

C. Safe Lessons: The Importance of Balance

Goal: For students to stand in the stirrups without losing balance.

Let's say you want to teach the posting trot. The student's long-term goal is to be able to stand and sit in rhythm with the horse. The immediate goal is to stand in the stirrups without losing balance.

Many students find the rising trot difficult at first. Either they cannot get out of the saddle, or they fall back into the saddle, or their hands flail the air, or they simply bounce roughly on the horse's back. To Western riders, beginning to sit a trot, as opposed to a smooth jog, is just as difficult; we start them the same way. Many Western horses do not have a smooth pleasure jog.

We see the student struggling and may say that the student doesn't know how to trot, or post, or sit, or whatever. But the real problem is that the student has not found his balance because he cannot keep his legs still and under himself and/or relax his lower back. But balance isn't the goal of the lesson; that skill seldom can be learned in one lesson.

Until the student can keep his legs under his body, he cannot control his hands, feet, or anything else. Our first major obligation, then, is to help the student control his legs. Once the rider can control his legs, he'll be able to find his balance and control his upper body, hence, his hands. So controlling the legs is the goal of this lesson — and of several more lessons.

Balance results when the rider's center of gravity is as close as possible to the horse's. That will be achieved when the rider is sitting completely relaxed in correct alignment.

The rider is in correct alignment when there is a straight, vertical line:

- **from the rider's ear**
- **to the shoulder**
- **to the point of the hip**
- **to the back of the heel.**

Beginning to sit a trot, as opposed to a smooth jog, can be just as difficult for a Western rider. Here, the student sits too far back in the saddle and is reaching for the stirrup with her toe.

Dick Pond

This line should usually be perpendicular to the horizon. The exception is in jumping or galloping cross country, when the upper body is inclined forward, but still balanced over the feet.

Is this alignment the goal? No. The student won't understand if you tell her to line up her ear, shoulder, hip, and heels. You can, however, ask her to arrange her body so that she can sit, stand, and sit again without the support of her hands. If she has to move her legs, they are in the wrong place. Start by asking the student to stand in the stirrups without support of the hands; then to stand and sit and stand; then to stand on the moving horse. Little goals are important so that students — adults and children — as well as instructors, can see results from **each and every lesson.** This is first done with support from the mane — not to hold the rider up, but to prevent a flop down on the horse's back.

The stretching exercises most instructors use also teach balance and leg position through muscle memory if the legs are kept in place throughout the exercise. Nonmounted exercises also help.

Examples
- Walking on heels
- Walking (later add running) with cups of water held in front of the body (as reins would be). Don't spill!
- Contact — practice holding the reins while a partner plays the part of the

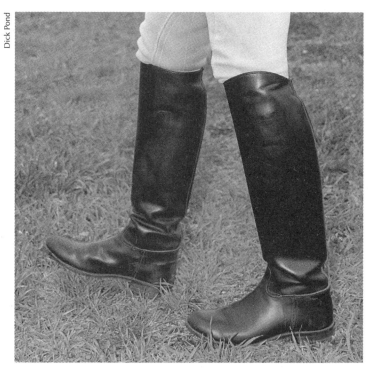

Unmounted exercises can help teach balance and leg position. One such exercise is to walk on the heels while keeping the body properly aligned. Another is to walk with a cup of water in front of the body — as a rider would hold reins. This student should be holding her hands a bit lower!

horse. The goal is to maintain a steady, light contact as the "horse" moves his head, then varies the movement.

Whether you are teaching a ring full of beginners — four to six riders — or a private lesson, students must have the rudiments of stopping, starting, and steering.

If you are teaching a longe lesson, you may go directly to the warm-up exercises that teach leg position, alignment, and sitting.

Parts of the lesson may be given as homework.

D. Sample Lesson Plan: Mounting

Goal: For students to learn the seven steps of a lesson plan.

When you are just beginning your teaching, your lesson plan for each session may be more detailed than it will be later. It may even be written down so you have all the parts. Try the explanation out on yourself. You will know if it works.

Your written plan for a mounting lesson would look something like this:

Mounting

Safety check — always, always, always

Introduction — why mounting is dangerous, what we must do to make it safe. Write your answers here if you had to look them up.

Review — relate mounting to the safety lecture: "What did we do to convince this grazing-type animal to let us get on?" Another little goal is to understand why the technique you are teaching is safer than some other way.

Goals/explanation/demonstration — the seven steps of mounting

Practice — seven steps, then 1-2-3-4

Summary — mounting, 1-2-3-4 vocabulary, and information: what we know about mounting. Remember, when you get to the summary, it must agree in content with the goals/explanation/ demonstration segments of the lesson.

E. Sample Lesson Plan: Skills Review Using Strategy Questions

Goal: For students to demostrate their understanding of their last lesson.

The pre-mounting part of early lessons should review all the skills covered in the first safety lecture — the instructor should be prepared to ask "why" and "why not" about all the skills. Students' regular responses turn into good habits. Don't forget to review weather, facility, student, horse, tack, cinch/girth.

Make anything a question; then ask why. That way, the students learn not only the skill, but also why it is important. They should be able to relate their "why" answers back to the initial safety lecture — if that initial lecture was adequate. The student should be prepared to respond with the answer and the "why" to the following questions and any others you can think of.

These can be a rainy-day quiz or a ground school.

SAMPLE STRATEGY QUESTIONS

These will get your students to **think, recall, and use** information.

1. **Basic Safety**
    a. Why do we wear hard hats?
    b. If we're just grooming the horses, is it OK to leave off the helmet?
    c. What about loafers — is it OK to wear loafers or running shoes to ride?
    d. How about sandals to work around horses?
    e. I saw a girl on TV riding in shorts — is that OK?
    f. Does a good rider chew gum while riding? Why not?
    g. Is it OK to tie your horse and go to get a drink?
    h. What is a safety check? What do we check and why?

2. **Approaching horses**
    a. You are in a hurry, so what about running up to the horse?
    b. What if I talk to my horse and his ears don't move? Should I go ahead and pat him?
    c. Should you walk up to a horse's shoulder in a tie stall?
    d. Can I go into the box stall when his tail is to the door?
    e. Why should you never approach from the front or the rear?
    f. Your horse really likes apples. Should you give him the rest of yours?

3. **Handling horses**
    (I have included responses to these sample questions.)
    a. Star is super gentle, you don't need a lead rope, do you?
       Yes, you do, not only to tie her, but also because she could easily be startled, get away, upset someone else's horse, and cause an accident.
    b. I'm left-handed. May I lead my horse from the right side?
       No. What if the horse is not accustomed to that? Might he be nervous and step on you?
    c. It's easier for me to hold the clasp on the rope attached to the halter than it is to hold the rope, and the rope is wet, anyway.
       What if your horse jerks away?
    d. My new lead rope will get dirty on the ground. I'll just put my arm through the loops for a couple of seconds while I halter Star. Is that OK?
       Never, ever, put your hand or arm through the loops of rope or longe line. You could get caught up and dragged if the horse takes off.

F. Sample Lesson Plan:
Overall Plan for a Package of Lessons

This type of plan is important for the instructor whose students are enrolled for a specific series of lessons, such as a one-week or two-week camp session or a riding stable's 10-lesson package. It is a good idea for any instructor, as the "Overall Plan" allows her to view her subject in units.

The camp instructor may arrange her Overall Plan in terms of her one-week time limit. The riding stable instructor might arrange her Overall Plan in terms of the skills required to achieve various Certified Rider patches or the skills necessary for beginning jumping or trail riding. Here is an example of a plan for a 10-lesson package. This will be ambitious for group situations, but possible in private lessons.

Lesson 1. Initial safety lecture: the nature of the horse and why he can be dangerous. Remember to keep to the lesson format as much as possible. Ask students to explain how a horse would react in different situations. In the summary, aim for the important principles: predator/prey, flee/flight, and responses to pressure.

Important Principles
- The horse is a prey animal.
- The horse is a herd animal.
- Demonstrate approaching, haltering, leading, tying.
- Demonstrate equipment safety check.

You'll need to abbreviate to get all this into one lesson.

Lesson 2. Demonstrate saddling and bridling. Teach mounting and dismounting; standing and sitting; correct alignment.

Lesson 3. Aids for walk, halt, and turns. Emergency stop. Start, stop, turn right, turn left; circle, half circle.

Lesson 4. Emergency dismount and stop (see Chapter 12); school figures at walk — figure 8 and serpentine.

Lesson 5. First balance lesson at walk: Touch ears, tail, toes; stand in stirrups — all with seat in saddle and legs in correct position (this is why we do these exercises).

Lesson 6. Review previous exercises and:
Goal 1: Stand in stirrups without hand support
Goal 2: Stand in stirrups without hand hold at walk
Goal 3: Stand, sit, stand without hand support
Goal 4: Goal 3 at walk (make sure this is done with toes pointed up and heels down, when standing, not with legs away from horse or pushed forward)

Lesson 7. Review exercises: Review emergency stop; aids for trot; review stand, sit, stand at walk.
Goal 1: To sit a few steps of trot
Goal 2: Stand in stirrups with support at trot

Lesson 8. Review previous exercises: emergency stop; aids for trot; stand with support at trot; emergency dismount.
Goal: Stand, sit, stand in rhythm with horse at least five steps

Lesson 9. Review previous exercises: emergency stop; aids for walk and trot; stand, sit, stand at walk; stand, sit, stand at trot with a little support
Goal: Stand, sit, stand in rhythm for 10 steps — or rising or posting trot

Lesson 10. Review previous exercises

Goal of the unit: Posting or rising trot with correct legs and body

Each instructor's Overall Plan may be different. It's only important that the plan be realistic and the goals attainable. Each lesson should build on the one before and lay the groundwork for the one following.

Lesson plans should not be written in stone. The safe instructor may decide that her students need to repeat all or part of a previous lesson. To do this, she may have them play a game that utilizes the skills needing attention. The important thing to understand is that each lesson must be tailored to the abilities of the current student or students. We must be ready to adapt our plans so that our goals are attainable by the students we see that day, in that situation. We must avoid accepting substandard skills that students will have to unlearn or relearn later.

We may have to rewrite our plan before we get to the arena or even after, due to:
• **Weather conditions**
• **Students' attitudes**
• **Horses' attitudes**
• **Temporary distractions in the arena**
• **Insufficient grasp of previous lesson**

Sometimes, a lesson plan will fail because the instructor fails to manage the class well. The poorly managed class is an unsafe class.

Horseback riding is a sport requiring a great deal of discipline if it is to be done safely. Students who talk or cut up during a class make learning difficult for the others. They also make the class unsafe. Disruptive students should be dropped from the class or removed until such time as they decide to follow instructions.

This rule sometimes must be invoked even with adults. No instructor should be afraid to remove an adult from a class when the safety or learning of the others is at stake.

It is also poor management to group students of different abilities together in the same class. Classes should be sorted out based on students' abilities. This is where an Overall Plan again can really be of help. With such a plan, the instructor has a better idea of what is meant at her facility by "beginner," "intermediate," and "advanced." At one stable "advanced" may be the same as "advanced beginner" or "intermediate" at another. The labels are not important, but the instructor must see her students in terms of their abilities.

In a beginner class, one student may progress more rapidly than the others. Such a student should also be removed and placed in another class so as not to hold her back or bore her into carelessness. The same is true of the student who does not progress as rapidly as the others.

Under no circumstances should an instructor ridicule the less talented students or use the more talented students to make the others feel uncomfortable. The instructor's job is to teach safe riding and safe horse management to all the students.

Before each lesson, the safe instructor will run through the following checklist to make sure everything is as safe as possible for riding:

- ✔ *Condition of each horse:* Look for signs of lameness, illness, or attitude.
- ✔ *Condition of student:* Attitudes of fear or overconfidence or a temporary illness or preoccupation can affect the lesson.
- ✔ *Condition of tack:* Check all stress points — girths, cinches, reins, latigos. Tack and cinches will be checked several times.
- ✔ *Condition of facility:* Are there any hazards, open gates, new distractions, baby strollers, strange dogs?
- ✔ *Condition of weather:* If it's hot and humid, take alcohol/water (1 qt. rubbing alcohol in 5 gal. bucket of water) to the ring to sponge on horses, and drinking water for the riders; if it's cold or there's an impending storm with a dropping barometer, maybe it's better not to ride; lightning — don't ride; darkness — are the lights adequate?

1. Name and describe the five components of a riding lesson. (page 62)

2. A good instructor always has a _____. The _____ always has a _____. The _____ is measurable. The_____ student can reach the _____. (page 62)

3. Distinguish among *goal and subskill* in the first mounting lesson. (page 64)

4. True or False: A student who has been properly taught to mount correctly will know why some horses fidget and refuse to stand while being mounted. (page 65)

5. Until the student can keep his _____ still under his body, he cannot control his _____. (page 67)

6. Balance is achieved when the rider's _____ of _____ is as close as possible to the horse's. (page 67)

7. Describe two exercises for still hands and light contact. (pages 68-69)

8. Write a sample lesson plan for dismounting. (page 69)

9. Give an example of strategy questions for a review of a mounting lesson. (page 70)

10. Give three reasons why lesson plans fail. (page 72)

TEACHING SAFE LESSONS

Having grown up with Hollywood cowboys — or worse, unskilled neighbors with horses or with friends who ride but have never had lessons — many parents and students have difficulty understanding the danger. We as instructors may seem paranoid to them. Many students are overconfident. That is easy to deal with — a few early exercises will take care of that problem. Just give the overconfident student an exercise or question or two and let the challenge be his reality check.

A. Safety Ground School

Safe lessons begin with the safety ground school discussed in Chapter 2. Some instructors do this with a videotape. We don't recommend using tapes, because they are not as effective as direct communication between teacher and student.

The first contact with the student and a parent is an opportunity to explain to the student and parent why safety is stressed and why we must have so much respect for the horse. We always use the "Nature of the Horse" lecture as our starting point. A parent should be present if possible for the safety ground school (have a sign-in sheet to keep for your files).

The fearful student will gain confidence as she understands the horse and learns that some behaviors are predictable and that some unpredictable behaviors can be controlled. As she feels more secure, and her abilities grow, confidence will come. Teaching control, both of a situation and of the horse itself, is important. If students learn how bad situations can develop, they will avoid them. If they understand how unpredictable behaviors can be controlled, they will practice their control skills willingly. Practiced skills become habit.

IN THIS CHAPTER

Safety Ground School

Control Skills

Safety Skill Levels

Starting Beginners

The 7-7-7 Exercise

B. Control Skills

The **emergency stop** and the **ability to turn** the horse who doesn't want to turn require a secure seat. Therefore, the instructor first must teach the student how to sit securely and that position faults will cost her that security.

When all else fails, the student must know that she can safely get off whenever she wants: **the emergency dismount.** (See Chapter 12.)

C. Safety Skill Levels

Many instructors with years of teaching experience are not able to say exactly what a particular student can safely do at any given time. They also are forced to give vague answers when a student asks, "When can I canter or lope?" "When can I jump?" "When can I go on the trail?" (More about this appears in the next chapter.)

The instructor must have it well set in her mind what skills are involved. It is a bad idea to rely totally on the "gentleness" or "predictability" of the horse, although on most guest ranches and in many beginner lessons, that is exactly what is done.

D. Starting Beginners

We recommend that beginners be started on a longe line in a round pen or small corral, but only by an instructor who is **highly skilled in longe-line teaching.** This, however, may not be feasible, as that requires that each beginner be started in private lessons by an instructor with many years of experience and highly advanced skills. Therefore, it is imperative that beginner groups be small — not more than four appropriate students, with an assistant instructor.

An instructor should have enough experience to see an accident getting ready to happen and stop it before it does. For example, notice a change in spacing immediately. Notice a rider leaning to one side, and especially notice a leg out of position. Notice a horse beginning to think about spooking. See a hazard coming that will spook the class. Get them off the horses if you must. When longeing is not advisable, then beginners should be taught in a small area so the horses don't get the idea that they must "catch up," or go find their buddies, or that they can have a good gallop. The area also must be large enough to maintain safe spacing with a little maneuvering room left over.

E. The 7-7-7 Exercise

Although most beginner lessons are taught by the old "start, stop, and steer" method, it is better to teach the student to sit securely and correctly and then how to refine the stop, steer, and start as quickly as possible. If the balanced seat is taught by a series of related exercises, not only will the instructor be able to analyze the student's seat or position and make adjustments at any time, but also the student will learn to do this for himself and it will be natural, not a posed position that results in dangerous stiffness. The student can then, whenever neccessary, go back to the exercises and regain a temporarily lost balanced seat.

Further, if the instructor is competent to teach the rudiments of jumping, the student will feel more secure and will be more secure if she learns to negotiate small obstacles. You can't and shouldn't try to teach a horse to shy in order to teach a secure seat, but you can teach a student to jump.

The same exercises can be used with either Western or English riders. We recommend teaching the rising trot and the two-handed rein to all beginners, even Western riders. Just tell them most Western trainers ride two-handed at home — most of them do! As I've explained earlier, probably there is a bias in this handbook for starting beginners on English saddles because if the student falls off she will less likely be hung up on an English saddle.

Only a brief discussion of the basic exercise is included here — more details appear in Chapter 9. It is imperative that the instructor understand this exercise fully and be able to perform it well, or have someone available who can demonstrate it if the instructor is no longer able.

We start Western as well as English riders with the two-handed or direct rein, as shown here.

The 7-7-7 Exercise

- 7 strides sitting trot
- 7 strides rising trot (Western, too)
- 7 strides standing or "light seat" or "two-point position"

A balanced rider will have a secure upper body (left) and will be able to stand in her stirrups without moving her secure lower legs (right).

This exercise will teach the rider to move the upper body around over a correctly placed leg that stays put. If the leg is wrong, the rider can't do the exercise. The various things that can go wrong will tell the instructor and the student exactly where the problem lies.

The student also learns to check her seat constantly by standing slightly and staying up. If she can't stand up without moving her leg, it is in the wrong place.

Remember, a steady, correct leg produces a quiet, secure upper body, which produces quiet hands that can softly control the horse. **We build the seat from the leg up.**

Chapter 8 — Review Questions

1. A parent should be present at the first "Nature of the Horse" lesson. Why? (page 75)

2. Before we can teach students maneuvers such as the emergency stop, we must teach them to have a secure _____. (page 76)

3. If students learn how bad situations can develop, they will _____ them. If they learn how unpredictable behavior can be controlled, they will practice their _____ skills. (page 75)

4. Even though we acknowledge that the longe line is the best place to start beginners, we do not recommend that everyone do it this way. Why not? (page 76)

5. An instructor should have enough experience to_____ an accident before it happens and _____ it. (page 76)

6. Give two reasons why it is better to teach balanced seat through exercises. (pages 76-77)

7. True or False: Exercises are the same for Western and English styles of riding. (page 77)

8. True or False: Teaching each student some basic jumping is preferable to teaching the horse to shy. (page 77)

9. True or False: The 7-7-7 exercise teaches the rider to move the upper body around over a stationary, correct leg, thus developing the leg as an anchor. (pages 77-78)

10. We build the seat from the top down/bottom up (Circle one). (page 78)

Teaching from Interrelated Lesson Plans

No one ever learned to ride a horse by being told where to put his body parts in space. At AAHS headquarters, we use a series of balancing exercises to help the rider develop the correct leg position as quickly as possible. A correct leg leads to a correct seat and the two together keep the student from falling off and free the student's hands to control the horse. Here in the form of several lessons plans are the exercises that we use to teach security on a horse and to evaluate a rider's basic position.

A student's ability or inability to do the mainstay 7-7-7 exercise will give the instructor not only a fair idea of the rider's ability, but also specific information as to what the rider needs to do to be more secure. It also allows the instructor to give the student specific answers to such questions as: "When can I lope?" "When can I jump?" or "When can I get off the longe line or out of the round pen?" The instructor simply sets the skills at a level comfortable for her. "You will get out of the round pen when you can do the 7-7-7 exercise without hands on the neck." There is the goal and the motivation.

A. Lesson Plan I

This lesson is appropriate when the students have developed a bit of a feel for a sitting trot and a fairly vertical two-point — they can stand a few strides at the trot.

1. Introduction

Begin with the rising trot — some call it "posting trot." English riders use this frequently; Western riders use it often to ride a long or rough trot or simply to cover long distances; it is easier on the horse.

2. Review

We have learned the aids to make the horse go forward. Who can tell me what they are? (When you ask a specific student a question, say the name last or else the others may not listen.) What are they for turning right? For turning left? We will warm up with a series of transitions — walk to halt to walk — and then with Mary in the lead, we will review the school figures. The students may be doing their warm-ups.

3. Goal/Explanation/Demonstration

Who knows what a posting trot is? Right, it's standing and sitting in time to the horse's movement. (Demonstration.) What has to happen for you to be able to stand up? Can your feet be out in front of you? No, of course not. You can't get up, or you fall back. What about if your feet are too far back? Right, you will fall forward.

So your feet have to be under you, just as if you were standing on the ground. (The subskill is to stand up in stirrups; the goal is to stand up in stirrups and sit down in rhythm with the horse.)

4. Practice

So let's try it one at a time — all the rest can watch and analyze (they are all walking on the rail). Who will be the first guinea pig? (Just a few strides, with the instructor counting 1, 2, 1, 2 or calling "up, down, up, down." The student trots around the rail to the back of the class.)

The rider's lower leg is too far forward.

Common Mistakes
- Lower leg too far forward
- Using reins for balance
- Rising from stirrups instead of heels
- Rising too high
- Flopping back too hard
- Lack of rhythm

5. Summary Questions

"What did you learn? What problems did you have? Can you think of an on-the-ground exercise you can practice for next time?" (They can walk on their heels with a straight back, not leaning over.)

Note: The student will not be able to rise out of the saddle unless his feet are correctly placed under him for support. The student should allow the horse's movement to push him up; a **light** grip with his calf will help. He should have weight in his heels and use his ankles and knee joints to soften his return to the saddle. It is better for a student to support himself at the beginning with a handful of mane rather than hitting the horse in the mouth or flopping on his back while learning. On the other hand, watch out for students who are chronic "mane hangers," because they are not in balance nor will they find balance.

It is better for a student to support himself at the beginning with a handful of mane than hitting the horse in the mouth or flopping on his back while learning.

Caution: The students must be able to do the warm-ups at the walk and stand and sit at the walk or they *will not* have the skills to do this exercise.

B. Lesson Plan II

This lesson is appropriate after students have successfully mastered all the skills and subskills in Lesson Plan I.

1. Introduction

"Today we will introduce the two-point or light seat — or galloping position. It is the mainstay of early riders because if we can stand with our weight in our heels and joints flexed, we can ride out most early problems. Why? Because it keeps us in correct alignment; joints are flexed so there is no stiffness that might cause a tumble. Our joints serve as shock absorbers."

2. Review

"Last time, we worked on posting (rising) trot. Let's see what you remember, one at a time" (go to the previous summary for this).

3. Goal/Explanation/Demonstration

"Two-point is what happens at the top or 'up' count of the rising trot, except you have to stay there, and eventually you should stay there without holding on." (Demonstrate: Ride the rising trot, then stay up off the saddle several strides, and repeat so that students can see the difference. Use a student's horse, as you should not be mounted for the lesson. You may have an assistant, an advanced student, or a working student or intern available to do the demonstration.)

4. Practice

"Stand in your stirrups and let your weight sink to your heels, with flexed knee, hip, and ankle. Stand and sit a few times. Support yourselves with the mane." (Falling forward tells you and them that their feet are too far back; if they must hold the mane to keep from sitting down, their feet are too far forward. Give students this information so they can hunt for the balance point themselves.)

Students must experiment with leg positions until they find their balance, first at the walk and then at the trot, one at a time. If the student comprehends the importance of the leg position, this becomes a diagnostic or self-regulating exercise.

Common Mistakes
- Using mane to maintain position all the time
- Standing on toes
- Leaning too far forward over a leg that is too far forward
- Eyes down — consequently, rider's back is round, chest is hollow, and rider is out of balance

5. Summary Questions

"What was learned?"

"What do you know if we fall forward? back? can't get up? Why must we use the mane while we're learning?

C. Lesson Plan III

This lesson is appropriate after students have successfully mastered all the skills and subskills in Lesson Plan II.

1. Introduction

"We will sit at the trot, paying particular attention to the horse's movement."

2. Review

"After your warm-up exercises, we'll do some walk-halt transitions, then I want to see what you learned last time. Who wants to tell me what that was? What must we watch out for on rising trot and two-point?"

3. Goal/Explanation/Demonstration

The students can watch horses and see that the horse does not use both hind (or front) feet at the same time. (Direct their attention to the trot. Students will notice that the horse's back moves as each hind foot steps forward.) Demonstrate the trot in two-point, showing how the movement of the horse shifts the relaxed rider's weight from side to side. (The demonstrator must be able to perform this. The weight drops into the stirrup as the hind leg on that side leaves the ground.) The instructor — whoever is doing the demonstration — then sits the trot, remaining so relaxed that the horse's movement goes on through the rider's body and shifts the rider's seat from side to side. It looks pretty funny at first, but students will learn that it is not necessary to grip to sit the trot, but to **relax.** Gripping squeezes the rider up and out of the saddle. Students must be cautioned to keep hands still when they sit. They may have already done the exercise of walking and running with a cup of water in each hand to learn to still their hands.)

When a student cannot keep her seat in the saddle, usually it is because she does not come back to true vertical alignment — ear *over* shoulder over hip — or because she has stiffened or locked her lower back.

4. Practice

One at a time, allow the students who are secure enough in their two-point with weight shifting side to side to try the two-point to sitting trot. Others may do two-point rising transitions.

Common Mistakes

- The student's two-point is too far forward, so when she sits, she is still too far forward and cannot sit the trot. In this case, the rider's legs are probably too far forward as well.
- The student grips with her knees or thighs, which raises her out of the saddle and does not allow her to relax and sit deeply. She also may lose her stirrups, because pinching with the knee draws up the leg.
- The student's hands fly around when she sits, which tells the instructor that the seat is not secure, the legs are moving, and the back is stiff. Go back to the rising two-point combinations and then come back to the two-point, while shifting weight side to side from heel to heel and try sitting again with the funny, totally relaxed body.
- The student flops down in the saddle instead of lowering herself straight down and relaxing. Emphasize "lowering" the seat into the saddle rather than letting go, which results in "flop and hop." The student must simply bend her knees and let the seat bones go straight down into the saddle.

5. Summary Questions

"What did you learn today? What happened if you pinched with your knee? What happened if you were too far forward in your two-point? How about too far back? Who will explain the two-point to sitting to two-point transitions?"

D. Lesson Plan IV

This lesson is appropriate after students have successfully mastered all the skills and subskills in Lesson Plan III.

1. Introduction

The students now have all the parts of an exercise that can be a self-diagnostic tool for the position for quite a while. We call this exercise the 7-7-7. You can use 8-8-8 if you want them to stay on the same diagonal. It puts together the rising trot, two-point, and sitting trot and will give the student a fairly secure seat and correct leg. It will also allow the instructor quite quickly to measure accurately the progress of beginners (and the balance and flexibility of the more advanced).

BASIC WARM-UP

When we refer to the "basic warm-up," we refer to 10 reverse arm circles with each arm; touch ears with each hand while keeping the seat in the saddle and legs in place; sliding each hand over the rump and touching the tail while looking at the tail and keeping legs in place; touching left toe with left hand with legs in place; touching right toe with right hand with legs in place; touching left toe with right hand with legs in place; touching right toe with left hand with legs in place.

Each, except the arm circles, is repeated five times.

These exercises for the rider should begin every lesson. The 7-7-7 is then added to these exercises. The 7-7-7 exercises require the students to demonstrate all of the skills required by an independent, balanced seat.

Remember: When teaching beginner-class lessons, it is necessary to teach students to turn and to do school figures at the walk. They should be able to sit and stand and stay standing several strides at the walk before the trot is attempted. They also should have learned the emergency stop and dismount so they really are comfortable at the walk. Stress the correct leg and be careful that students don't confuse "heels down" with "jam the heel and lower leg forward." We say, "point the toe up" or "drag heels in the dirt under the horse" to avoid the heel being held too far forward. The heel needs to be down only slightly at the walk, as we want weight in the seat. If the student is ready to progress farther, he should be able to do the 7-7-7 correctly, indefinitely, without support from the neck of the horse.

A rider doing the basic warm-up should keep her legs in place while touching the tail.

1.

2.

This rider is touching her left toe with her right hand with legs in place. In the first photo (1), the rider's upper-body position is too far forward during the toe-touch. The second photo (2) shows the correct upper-body position.

At AAHS headquarters, we use this exercise to tell us when our longe-line beginners are ready to ride alone. If they can do this exercise, their position is secure enough for them to learn to stop, steer, and perform an emergency stop well.

We use the same exercises with beginner classes, but it takes longer when a student must learn two skills at once: to balance on the horse and to control the horse. If the leg is out of place, the student cannot complete the exercise.

By analyzing the problems, the instructor can better help the student protect the correct leg position, which will keep the student on the horse.

2. Review

Use questions and demonstrations from Plan III. Ask the students, who by now can trot as a group — or in two groups, if you have an assistant — to demonstrate the parts of the 7-7-7. The students can now add the 7-7-7 exercise to their basic warm-up.

3. Goal/Explanation/Demonstration

Students will put the three parts together for the first time in a repeated 7-7-7 sequence.

Repeated 7-7-7 Sequence
- 7 strides (count on one fore foot, not each step of both) of rising trot
- 7 strides of 2-point
- 7 strides of sitting
- *Repeat*

The demonstration should show the exercise done correctly and then show what happens when body parts are out of place.

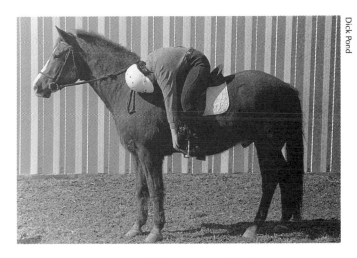

This rider's head should be closer to her knee.

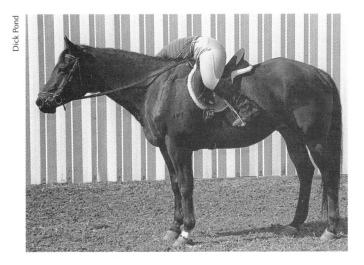

At left, the rider's legs have slipped too far back during the toe-touch to the right. At right, notice how the legs should remain when the exercise is done correctly.

4. Practice

The students can practice on the rail, while the instructor helps them find the alignment and balance individually. It is not a fault or error to practice any two segments by themselves that are particularly troublesome or to provide better preparation for a more difficult part.

Common Mistakes
- Depending on the mane
- Compensating for an incorrect leg by gripping to hold yourself up
- Leaning too far forward
- Leaning forward while sitting when you must have the ear over the hip
- Pushing the lower leg forward rather than heels to the ground

5. Summary Questions

The students can analyze their efforts and explain what they need to correct. Ask them to answer specific questions: "What happens if you . . . ? What do you know when . . . ?"

1. A correct leg leads to a correct _____. (page 79)

2. True or False: The 7-7-7 exercise will test the rider's skills and tell the instructor where the problems are. (page 79)

3. When you ask a student a question, say the name _____. (page 80)

4. True or False: The review is the instructor's best opportunity to see if the previous lesson was learned or needs more work. (page 81)

5. Why is it better to ask the students to summarize than for you to do it for them? (page 86)

6. If the answer to the question, "What was this lesson about?" is "Hmmmmm," what does that tell the instructor? (See question 5 above.) (page 86)

7. True or False: By analyzing problems with the 7-7-7 exercise, the instructor can help the student correct her leg position. (page 85)

8. Who should demonstrate the skills to a beginner class? List the three possibilities. 1)_____ 2)_____ 3)_____ (page 81)

9. Below are some common mistakes encountered during a 7-7-7. What are their causes? (pages 80-83)

    Can't get out of saddle _____

    Must hold mane to stay up _____

    Cannot sit trot _____

    Fell forward onto hands _____

    Loses stirrups when sits _____

    Hands fly around _____

    Lower leg too far forward _____

10. The heel only needs to be down slightly at the walk (and sitting trot) because _____. (page 84)

SAMPLE INTERMEDIATE LESSON PLANS

Always, always have a plan. Think through everything. Just as the horse is the trainer's teacher, the student is the instructor's teacher. If we ask the horse to perform a task and he performs incorrectly, we must rephrase the request. The horse usually thinks he is doing what was asked. It is the same with the student. *If the student responds incorrectly, rephrase the instructions.*

A. Intermediate Lesson Plan I

The instructor employs the same safeguards with intermediate students that she does with beginners.

1. Introduction

"Today, we begin the canter or lope. This is a three-beat, asymmetrical gait in which the horse moves as follows: outside hind, inside hind, and outside fore together, inside or leading leg."

Right Lead		Left Lead	
②	③	③	②
①	②	②	①

2. Review

The student has learned the aids to the walk and trot. She can sit the trot, post or rise to the trot, and maintain a two-point position in the trot. She can perform the school figures and now can warm up with the school figures. She can go from sitting to rising to 2-point easily without support from her hands. And she can trot cavalletti (ground poles, about three feet apart — distance may vary among horses) with a cross pole at the end. Review all this in the warm-up. The student is now ready to begin canter work. She probably already will have cantered a little as a result of the cross pole, and this is good. She has felt canter and learned how to return to the halt.

3. Goal/Explanation/Demonstration and Teaching Suggestions

The goal for the day is a few strides of canter on any lead. The instructor is now moving into one of the high-risk areas. Many students take a tumble at this stage because they canter too soon. They may not be hurt, but they certainly can be frightened. Often students fall at this stage because they canter too long. Any fall can result in serious injury. It probably won't, but it can. The position falls apart, and off they go. So when students canter for the first time, they should have the following protection. (If this canter is on a longe line, it will be covered in the section on longeing. Be sure to read that whole section before attempting to longe a rider.)

Safety Precautions for Teaching the Canter

- Only one student at a time should attempt the canter.
- The canter should be only for a short distance, as from one end of the class in a small ring to the other end. Five or six strides is plenty to start.
- The horses should have a fairly smooth, short gait and a willing stop.
- The canter should be attempted only in a small area, after a good warm-up of both horse and rider during which the instructor can spot any problems.
- If the student cannot do a secure 7-7-7 with a stationary leg, she is not ready to canter. Remember, the 7-7-7 exercise is seven strides sitting trot, seven strides rising trot, and seven strides two-point position. Even students headed for Western riding should be able to do this. Many Western showring trainers use a variation of this exercise for their youth horsemanship contestants.

It is worthwhile to start even your "wanna-be" Western riders on flat saddles simply because they will be able to feel more, and they will gain considerable security by doing cavalletti and small (one- to two-foot) obstacles. In addition, even as

Horses will offer a canter after jumping a small cross pole.

Students learning to canter should do so only one at a time, and only for a short distance.

Western riders, they may need to be able to stay with (that is, on top of and in the middle of) a horse who jumps a small creek or log rather than stepping over it. Some Western trail classes contain small jumps. Often when a horse jumps a small obstacle, the insecure rider may interfere with the horse to the extent that the horse is spooked by the rider's clumsiness.

4. Practice

Students can take turns cantering to the end of the line both ways. The instructor makes sure the student's position is most like sitting trot with a steady leg.

5. Summary Questions

Why do we canter one at a time? Describe the gait of the canter. (The instructor may use any question that will draw a response that tells her the lesson has been absorbed.)

B. Intermediate Lesson Plan II

Students continue to polish their cantering skills.

1. Introduction

"Today we will continue to work on cantering."

2. Review

"Last time, we learned the footfalls of the canter. Who can tell me what they are? We each cantered a little. How does it feel different from the trot?"

3. Goal/Explanation/Demonstration

"The goal today is to canter around the ring to the end of the line of riders — or to the instructor." (The instructor needs to explain and demonstrate the aids to canter clearly. It may also be helpful to demonstrate what happens when the aids are used incorrectly.) Years ago, students were told to put the horse's head to the rail and ask for the canter with the outside leg, which was placed slightly more behind the girth or cinch. This method has, for the most part, dropped out of favor as the horse would fall into his canter on the desired lead but off balance.

Now we prefer to keep the horse straight or on a circle, put slight tension on the outside rein for two-handed riders — or lift the hand slightly for Western riders — and bump the horse with the outside leg slightly behind the cinch, keeping the inside leg at the cinch. It is also correct to place the outside leg behind the cinch to control the haunches and ask with the inside leg, but I would not suggest that to a beginner. (It is important that the student learn on a horse who is willing to canter and especially helpful if the horse pretty much takes the correct lead. At this stage, it is more confusing than helpful to have the students worry about leads. They should worry only about developing the correct aids or cues. If this work is done on a circle on reliable horses, leads will never be a problem because the student will learn to tell what is correct. If the horse takes the wrong lead, except in the showring, do not punish him by bringing him harshly down immediately — allow him to canter a few strides, then gently bring him down and ask again for the canter, but more clearly. You asked for canter and got it, so don't try for revenge.)

4. Practice

Continue one at a time, then two at a time **only** if both students are secure. Students may canter on circles, large enough to accommodate the horse's stride, about 20 meters or 66 feet.

5. Summary Questions

"Who can explain the aids or cues for cantering" **(at this stage, it must be kept simple)**. "What is the sequence of footfalls for the canter? What went well with your practice attempts? What went poorly? What will you do differently next time?"

Common Mistakes
- **The student's aids or cues to the horse are not clear, so the horse only trots faster in response to the increased leg.** The student is probably asking with both legs instead of one; reins may be too long. The student may be leaning forward.
- **The horse veers suddenly into the circle at the trot instead of going ahead at the canter.** The student is asking too much with one leg and not using the other one at all, so the horse thinks he is supposed to turn in. The student might also have lost her balance, or forgotten to use the reins.
- **The horse canters a stride, then trots or walks.** The student is probably being caught off balance due to an out-of-position leg and is raising his hands when the horse tries to canter.

The goal is to canter when the student is ready. The first canter should be done reasonably well if the student was reasonably well prepared — by the instructor.

Note: It is perfectly permissible to canter one at a time in a circle at one end of the arena, but always ask for the canter going into the short side of the arena. The canter can also be started in a corner of a wide arena as the horse goes into the corner. The important thing is that the horse feels contained.

1. True or False: You still need to have a lesson plan for intermediate or advanced riders even though they already have the basics. (page 88)

2. Who is often the instructor's best teacher? (page 88)

3. If the student responds incorrectly, you should (page 88)

    a) walk out of the arena

    b) threaten the student with bodily harm

    c) rephrase the instruction

4. What skills should be mastered before "officially" teaching the canter? (pages 88-89)

5. Most students will have already cantered because of an earlier activity; which one? (page 89)

6. Why do we canter one at a time? (page 89)

7. What are the footfalls of the canter? Right lead? Left lead? (page 88)

8. Why not teach leads now? (pages 90-91)

9. What could be the problem if the horse only trots faster? (page 91)

10. The horse canters, then trots; he doesn't seem to stay in a canter. What may be the problem? (page 91)

TEACHING HIGH-RISK ACTIVITIES

Many quality texts are available on how to ride in various styles. Whether you ride English, Western, or sidesaddle, "correct" means the same thing: The rider and horse are *in balance* and *in harmony*.

A. Balance

The horse and rider in balance make up a dynamic system; that is, both are in motion or they are preparing to be in motion together. The rider in balance with his horse is one not likely to be separated from his horse. To be in balance means that the rider's center of gravity is as close as it can get to the horse's center of gravity. The system works best if both parties are relaxed.

When the rider's center of gravity begins to drift away from the horse's, the rider's position becomes increasingly precarious, especially while jumping or at speed. As the balance or frame of the horse changes, so must the balance of the rider, if he is to remain secure.

The safe instructor understands that harmony with the horse means security for the rider. The safe instructor will not take the principles of equitation for granted. She knows that by so doing, she would put the student at risk. "Equitation" does not mean posing pretty on a horse.

B. High-Risk Advanced Teaching

As students progress, it will be necessary for the safe instructor to consider whether the more advanced students will need to learn competency at faster gaits out of the arena for such sports as eventing, competitive trail riding, reining, cutting, barrel racing or fox hunting to reach their goals. Here the instructor should use **extreme caution.** She must be competent to teach these skills. She must participate or have participated in the sports at a level above novice in order to teach them. For these activities, do not accept as students riders with a less-than-secure seat. If you do, you and the student are at risk. You may, however, accept the student and explain that you will first have to reengineer his seat before you can teach him to — whatever. Start him at the **beginning** and don't leave anything out. It may only take a month or a year or more.

Rules for Teaching High-Risk Activities
- No novice riders should be permitted to participate.
- Such training should be conducted only in a controlled situation: one student at a time, on a dependable horse, on safe terrain (one student on the course at a time).
- Because *galloping cross country, barrel racing, show jumping, team penning and cutting* by themselves invite accidents, it is *imperative* that the student have a very secure seat and experience in stopping and turning the horse at speed before attempting these skills.
- When first learning advanced skills, an older, well-trained, baby-sitter horse is essential.

It may be possible to accept as student a less-than-secure rider with his questionable horse who wants to be trained in a high-risk discipline. But a fall is predicable — and so is a lawsuit. No rule prevents you from sending this combination to someone else and letting them get sued instead.

C. The Longe Lesson

It is preferable to start all beginners — adults and children alike — on the longe line in a round pen or small corral. This is as effective for Western riders as it is for English riders. *This type of lesson should be taught only by an instructor experienced in longeing a rider and with a horse trained to longe.* It requires many hours of practice to be competent to teach on a longe line, so don't rush it. A year or more experience longeing horses in side reins is best before attempting to longe a rider.

1. Purpose
This type of lesson allows a student to develop an independent balanced seat in a highly controlled situation. The student can learn to be relaxed and move with the horse, following his movements. Performing a series of exercises, the student will learn suppleness, a deep relaxed seat, and have the ability to move his upper body over a correctly placed leg.

The instructor controls the horse, enabling the student to concentrate on balance. Equally important, the horse's sides and mouth are spared the student's uncoordinated bumping and thumping while she learns. *If we expect to communicate our wishes to the horse with our hands and legs, we must understand that all unnecessary movements will garble the message.* This can be a source of what often are called "dead-sided" and "hard-mouthed" horses.

2. For a Safe Longe Lesson You Need:

- An instructor experienced in use of the longe and in longeing riders. **No exceptions!**
- A set of side reins, preferably elastic — we are not training horses here.
- A strong longe line with a loop or disk at one end.
- Bridle with snaffle bit, either egg-butt or O-ring; a full cheek can tangle in the longe line. **Never longe with a curb bit.**
- Saddle well fitted to the student and horse. Don't compromise!
- A round pen 50 to 60 feet in diameter (preferred, but not essential) with even soft footing.
- A longe whip. Never touch the horse with the whip. It is used only to indicate that the horse should move forward.
- Most important, use a kind, calm, easy-moving older horse who is sound and has a gentle nature and is accustomed to longeing. Longe work is tiring, boring, and physically stressful for the horse. Not all horses are well suited for this job. **The horse should be reliably trained to voice commands, especially "Whoa." If you wouldn't be comfortable if another staff person longed you on the horse with your reins tied up and without stirrups, don't use that horse.**

The instructor must understand that in the event of a fall it is easy to pull the horse on top of the student while intending only to stop the horse. The "Whoa" command is imperative, and it is imperative that the horse respond **reliably** to it.

3. How to Prepare for a Safe Longe Lesson

Thorough preparation will increase the safety of a lesson.

- The instructor should tack the horse up normally with a snaffle bit and side reins, making sure that everything fits comfortably.
- Lead the horse to a restricted area where the other equipment has been placed. If a round pen or small corral is not available, choose the corner of an enclosed arena or small, level paddock with safe footing. Without a round pen, the instructor must be even more skilled and the horse more reliable. Make sure nothing will catch the rider's knee.
- In the longe area, attach the longe line by running the snap end through the bit ring on the inside, over the poll, and fasten it to the opposite outside ring. The line must be changed to reverse direction. This offers far more control than a longing cavesson. **Do not put your arm through the coiled longe line while making adjustments or changing direction! Not ever.** If you do it sometimes, you may do it by accident when the horse is attached. Hold the folds or tuck them under your arm.
- Attach the side reins and adjust them evenly and comfortably. Their purpose is to add stability and control — too loose or too tight can cause the horse to travel on his forehand, fight the bit, or flip over backward. Each horse will have a preference; too loose on one horse may be too tight on another. The rule of thumb is to attach the side reins so that the horse's nose is level with the point of his shoulders. First practice with each horse without the rider.

Remember, most of the time we are longeing beginners, not Olympians or bronc riders. We need a comfortable reliable horse, and we won't have one if we make his work too stressful.

- Always warm up the horse and longe him both ways in the side reins without the rider. The bridle reins should be tied up short in a knot and twisted under the throttle and secured by running the throat latch between them. The student should be outside the pen or area. **The reins should be freed from the throat latch before the rider mounts.** At this point, they can be tied in a knot out of the way, but where the rider can reach them.
- A safe instructor will concentrate on the horse while longeing without the rider. Ask these questions:
  - **a.** Is the horse sound and traveling freely?
  - **b.** When asked to stop, does he respond to "Whoa" immediately and settle into his bit?
  - **c.** If it is necessary to stop him with the longe line, does he fight the side reins or the bit? Are they adjusted comfortably? Too-tight side reins, especially on an unaccustomed horse, can cause a horse to run backward or, worse, to flip over. The horse must be steady, responsive, and stay out of the center of the longeing area unless you invite him in. If the horse acts uncomfortable, unsteady, or unruly, do not longe with him. If he is fresh, give him 10 to 15 minutes to settle down, but if you decide to use him, be very careful. A horse who will not stay out on the circle or will not readily follow voice commands (especially "whoa") is not a suitable longe horse. Remember, this is a *beginner* lesson.

When longeing a horse, don't count on help from the rider to keep the horse on a circle, because the rider is counting on you.

4. Characteristics of a Safe Longe Lesson
- The student should be instructed in mounting as for a regular lesson. An assistant is helpful because without one the instructor alone must manage the horse, longe line, whip, student, and mounting block.
- The reins must be freed from the throat latch and may be tied short in a knot.
- If the student is asked to hold the saddle at any time, it should be with two fingers of the outside hand under the pommel. This pulls the student forward and down into the saddle, affording the best balance and showing the student what a deep seat will feel like. Holding on is a good idea when the horse begins to move or when introducing a new gait. A strap connecting the two D-rings on the pommel may be purchased for about $20. My preference is two fingers under the pommel, rather than the "bucking strap."
- A safe instructor will use exercises to build the student's confidence, relax her body, and get her moving in harmony with the horse's movements. Exercises designed to challenge are best left for more advanced work.
- No movement should be used that might startle the horse. It is imperative that the longe horse be trained. That means he has experience being longed with riders who are doing exercises while he is moving. It requires two highly

experienced people to train a longe horse to be safe enough for beginners. Know your longe horse well. Ask an experienced staff person to longe you on the horse before you use him for longe lessons.

- A safe instructor will never ask a student to bend down to the outside of the horse without first bringing the horse away from the fence if longeing in a round pen or small corral.
- If the rider begins to lose her balance, the safe instructor will softly stop the horse and start over. This means loss of balance side-to-side, front-to-back — **any** such loss — start over. If the rider should topple off, stop the horse quietly. Note that it may have been your fault. *Remember,* a pull on the longe line brings the forehand in and takes the hindquarters out. If done too harshly, or abruptly, this can cause the horse to hit the side reins hard and back up. Any of these actions can bring the horse on top of the rider.
- Longe lessons are a good place to stabilize the rider's legs, so make sure that the student maintains correct leg position while doing exercises on the longe line.
- Always have the rider dismount in the center away from the fence, with the instructor holding the horse.

5. Some Hints for Longeing
- Because the instructor has control, the beginner rider can really concentrate on sitting and balance, so choose exercises that emphasize these skills.
- First build confidence, then relaxation, then skill.
- Never proceed to a more difficult exercise or a faster gait if there were difficulties with the previous one. Exercises should be done while maintaining a correct leg position and with the seat in the saddle. Don't slack off and let the rider do them any old way.

A new skill, if taught in the correct order, can be no better than the underlying skills. We train riders the way we train horses. Proper preparation means the new movement can be as well done as the previous movement. For instance:
- Give the longe horse frequent breaks and lots of praise — this is not an easy job for him.
- Never let a longe lesson last more than 30 minutes working time. Horses tire of this easily; they aren't carrying a quiet, well-balanced backpack, and the work is not interesting. Cold-blooded horses work best.
- Keep the lesson lively and the student busy — she will soon relax and find it easy or forget the fear if she is timid. Playing "Simon Says" rapidly directs the rider's mind away from the horse, and even the stiffest adult will relax — honest!
- Singing a round, such as "Three Blind Mice," can help with both rhythm and relaxation. Of course it feels silly, but it works, even with adults — especially with adults.
- Always be sure to change the longe line with each change of direction. Change directions frequently for the benefit of the horse.

6. What else is longeing good for?

- Your students can learn and practice the emergency dismount and stop on the longe line.
- Use of the aids can be safely learned with the instructor intervening less and less.
- Showing a student how to vary the horse's pace, frame, or to stop the horse completely all by seat and breathing alone is more easily accomplished on the longe line.
- Exercises on the longe line quickly show the student how to stay in the middle of the horse and where the seat bones are. She must put weight on the right seat bone to touch her left toe with her left hand when riding without stirrups. First, have the student imagine doing the exercise without stirrups. Later, you will have the student do them without stirrups. Many students will have to begin learning some of the exercises at a standstill until they work out the balance. It is best if they figure it out themselves, so avoid overcoaching. Exercises done without hands should not be done off the longe line.
- The teaching principles are the same on the longe line, but the student can learn much more quickly to influence with a seat that is independent of hands.

D. The Jumping Lesson

Do not attempt to teach jumping unless you, yourself, have had *formal* jumping training. That means lessons from a professional. If you jump and have not been formally trained, go to a certified jumping instructor for lessons and so that you can be coached in the teaching procedure, officially.

Jumping is a skill useful to all riders. The safe instructor knows she cannot teach the horse to shy, but learning basic jumping will help the student ride out a shying episode.

Equipment Guidelines for Beginning Jumping Lessons

- Jumping standards should be of stable construction, preferably tall enough to avoid impaling a rider — at least five feet.
- All jump cups not in *immediate* use should be removed to a safe place — not kept on the standards. This applies to pins, also.
- Place jumps away from other obstacles, including the fence.
- Beginning jumping lessons should be taught in a small, confined area that discourages horses from gaining undesired speed.
- A perimeter fence at least four feet high should enclose the beginner jumping area so that horses won't be tempted to leave the area or mistake the perimeter fence as another jump. Jumping can dislodge the beginner, who then will not be able to steer the horse very well even if he doesn't fall off. The perimeter fence must be safe to land on or topple onto — no strand wires, t-posts, or flags, or barbed wire.

- Cavalletti should be heavy enough not to roll when kicked or shatter when stepped on; 4-by-4 wood is best, but four-inch PVC will work, if the poles are at least 10 feet long. *Do not, however, use PVC for jump poles.* It is too easy to knock them forward and then land on them and fall. There are some PVC jumps made especially for that purpose. Use them with caution.

Remove jump cups and pins from standards when they are not in use.

- If wings are not used, the safe instructor will spend extra time making sure the students and horses are well schooled in going straight through the cavalletti and between the standards, not around them. At AAHS headquarters, we do not use wings or winged standards, because we want students to use their legs from the beginning.
- Nothing should be hanging from the standards or fences. That includes jackets, sweaters, and visitors.
- If there are dogs on the premises — and there usually are — keep them out of the riding area and especially the jumping areas.
- The gate must be closed.
- Approved safety helmets must be worn and checked for fit and tightness of the strap by hand; it may look snug, but it could be quite loose. Absolutely do not allow the use of unapproved headgear.

You may also want to consider requiring the use of protective jumping vests. The AAHS doesn't want to set a standard for this, but some stables now require vests for students as they move on to higher risk riding, such as jumping. More than one association now requires protective vests for cross-country riding. The use of these vests certainly affords some extra protection if riders have a spill; we at the AAHS, however, believe that although a must for cross-country riding and rodeo rough stock riding, they are not a substitute for a balanced, secure seat.

One Safe Way to Begin Jumping
- Nobody jumps without an approved helmet.
- Have students complete 30 minutes of correct warm-up exercises and school figures at the trot (or canter, where appropriate).
- While students are trotting, ask that they change from sitting to rising or posting trot to two-point (jumping or galloping position or light seat) and back to sitting trot (the 7-7-7) over and over. A student who can manage to change among rising, two-point, and sitting trot while keeping legs in place without losing his balance or rhythm should be prepared to begin jumping.
- The first jump: By the time the student sees her first cross poles, she should be proficient in riding at least a five-pole cavalletti without relying on support from the neck and with either arm held out to the side. A wobbly rider has

wobbly hands, which mean a wobbly bit, which means an uncomfortable and unsafe horse. You may assume wobbly legs with wobbly hands.

- The first jump is constructed by crossing the last two cavalletti in the lowest setting of the jump standards with the "X" only a few inches off the ground. A ground pole (a pole on the ground up against the bases of the cross poles) is advised, as with all jumps.

- The student should be asked to trot through the cavalletti, over the "X" while maintaining a correct two-point position, and stop on a straight line. He may be holding the mane or a jumping strap made by buckling a stirrup leather around the horse's neck. It is important to "stop on the line" so that horses will not develop the habit of ducking out to one side or the other after the jump — or speeding up.

- As the rider increases in skill, up to three elements may be added, 18 feet between the first and second and 19 feet between the second and third, depending on the individual horse's stride.

- Bounces, jumps with no stride between, 9 to 10 feet apart, help improve a student's elasticity, steadiness, and confidence. These also can be simple low cross poles. The instructor must have ridden the horse over the same type of obstacle before she attempts to teach a student to do it. A bounce can be created by adding a pole on the ground in the middle of an 18-foot one-stride; however, another cross pole is better, because a horse could step on a ground pole and fall.

- A safe instructor will be alert to differences in the school horses and adjust the distances accordingly. We are training riders, not horses.

- Combinations of more than three elements or heights greater that two feet six inches at the center are not for "beginners."

- It sometimes is helpful to have the rider say a cadence while approaching a jump to aid in keeping the rhythm, relaxing the body, and providing a checklist. An example, repeated in time to trotting or cantering strides, is offered below:

Eyes> Heels> Straight> Squeeze> Release

As soon as the student is straight to the jump, at least 36 feet out from it, he should lift his eyes from the center of the jump to a point on the far side of the line and count off:

Eyes> Heels> Straight> Squeeze> Release

- This is a cadenced reminder to look beyond the jump to a point beyond, put the heels down with weight in them, stay straight to the middle of the jump, squeeze gently with the inside of the calf just below the knee and don't let go, and release to the crest or a mane hold as the horse leaves the ground. The lower leg should be a bit more forward for jumping than on the flat, with the heels really down.

- Be sure the student doesn't try to take his leg off the horse to give him a kick. The horse may stop as the student takes his leg off to give that kick.

- It is extremely important that the student have a secure two-point position before jumping and that he is reminded to stay up and quiet throughout the jump. He should not try to jump for the horse. Jumping ahead of the horse or releasing too early (dropping) can cause a refusal. Most beginners have to learn to stay still, and they will approach their early jumps with a tight hold on the reins unless you remind them to release and grab the mane or neck strap. This prevents students from hitting the horse in the mouth or from flopping back. Getting left behind over a jump and hitting the horse in the mouth or flopping back on his kidneys doesn't make for a happy school horse. It's better to have a handhold.

Dick Pond

Dick Pond

Before attempting to jump, the student must be proficient at riding ground poles or a five-pole cavalletti without relying on support from the horse's neck. She should also be able to perform this exercise with one arm held out.

Cross the last two cavalletti into a low cross pole. The horse should trot into the jump, but sometimes will canter after the last cavalletti.

Carole Chiles Fuller

Dick Pond

Add a second cross pole 9 to 10 feet from the first to form a bounce.

It is very important that the student have a secure two-point position before jumping and that he is reminded to stay up and quiet throughout the jump. In this photo, the rider's center of gravity is directly over the horse's.

Teaching High-Risk Activities   **101**

- Always have the student halt the horse on a straight line after the jump. They should stand quietly a few seconds, then walk off. A horse that anticipates a halt does not anticipate running back to the group or charging away after a jump.

If You Still Don't Get It

Up to this point we have used lesson plans both to teach how to construct a lesson plan and to teach lessons about how to teach riding. That is how the basic skills must be taught in order to make the riders as safe as possible, to reduce the amount of time that they are most vulnerable, to do this with the least possible wear and tear on your good lesson horses, and to do it in a way that the rider is able to go back to a series of exercises and regain his skills after a break. But if you still don't get it, here is the MTV answer:

We talk to the horses by means of signals given through our hands, legs, seat, weight, and sometimes voice. If we just use our hands and legs to maintain our position on top of the horse, the horse won't be able to tell the difference: Are we communicating or just moving around trying to stay on?

To free the hands, legs, and seats for communication with the horse we must be able to maintain our position on top of the horse by balance alone. This means we must have what is called a "balanced seat." This can be taught to beginners of all disciplines. If it is not, someone will have to reteach the basics at some time if the rider ever desires to be even an accomplished pleasure rider. The correct (in any discipline) balanced seat rider is the least likely to fall off. She is also the least likely to spoil her or the stable's horse. As a result, the horse is less likely to hurt her.

In order to teach the balance or independent seat, the skills that make up the seat must be taught in a specific order. This is because the success of each skill depends on the quality of the underlying skill. The skills are taught by a series of specific exercises, because in order to remain relaxed (secure) the rider must discover his balance rather than being taught to pose in a specific position which is guaranteed to result in stiffness (risk of a fall).

The Skills and Their Accompanying Exercises

We'll say it one more time: This is how the basic skills must be taught to make riders as secure as possible, as quickly as possible.

1. Correct body alignment in which a vertical line perpendicular to the horizon would pass through the ear, shoulder point of the hip, and back of the heel of the rider.

    Exercise. The rider must be able to stand repeatedly without support from the hands, while maintaining this alignment first at the halt, then the walk, and then, eventually, at all three gaits.

2. Rider learns to move the upper body around over a stationary, correct leg.

    Exercise. Rider does arm circles, touches horse's ears, tail, and the rider's own toes on both sides with both hands while keeping her seat in saddle and her legs in place, first at the halt and then at the walk. Rider must keep weight centered, not all in one stirrup.

3. Rider learns to unlock lower back and move with the horse.

    Exercise. Rider pretends to sit in seat of bicycle, imagining the stirrups as pedals. Rider "pedals" backwards from the hips in rhythm with the horse.

4. Rider in correct alignment with stationary, relaxed leg unlocks the lower back and begins to move with the horse at the walk, and then trot.

    Exercise. Walk. Rider visualizes riding a bicycle, seated with feet on pedals and pedals backwards from the hips.

    Exercise. Trot. The 7-7-7 exercise emphasizing the lateral movement of the horse's back and relaxation of the rider's back.

5. The rider learns to survive sudden movements and avoid unwanted speed and faster gaits.

    Exercise. If the instructor is competent to do so **(has training and experience),** the rider can begin trotting poles on the ground (cavalletti) and then adding cross poles that are two feet high at the standards.

When the 7-7-7 exercise can be performed well indefinitely, even while riding the school figures, the rider has the basics of an independent balanced seat. At this point, the canter may be safely taught with no detrimental effects to the horse. Jumping beyond crosspoles can be taught.

If the rider is proficient in both the emergency dismount and emergency stop, she should be able to continue in the discipline or activity of her choice because she has the basic skills necessary to ride safely. The strong walk/trot rider with an emergency stop knows how not to canter and should be able to stay under control at all times.

In most situations it will be necessary to teach the start stop and steer skills as well. Do not waste this opportunity to teach correct school figures, or horsemanship patterns, or to teach a correct halt and up and down transitions from walk to halt.

Concentrate at all times on the lower leg and avoid going beyond a point where the rider has a well-positioned lower leg and is in fairly good balance.

Most falls occur because the rider loses his balance. In a lesson situation the instructor controls the degree to which a rider's balance is challenged.

Remember: All you really have to do is to teach the rider to keep one leg on each side of the horse at all times! This is easiest if the rider's heels are as close to the ground as possible at all times.

1. List four guidelines for high-risk teaching. (page 94)

2. To prepare to give a longe lesson:

    a. While adjusting equipment, place the longe line under your arm. Do not _____.

    b. Attach the side reins so that the horse's _____ is level with the _____.

    c. The danger with too-tight side reins is that_____.

    d. The horse should go quietly and respond to all commands, especially the voice command "_____." (pages 95-96)

3. A longe lesson should last no longer than _____ minutes. (page 97)

4. If you keep the longe lesson lively, the student will _____. (page 97)

5. Jumping standards should be at least _____ tall. (page 98)

6. Beginning jumping should be taught in a [large, small] arena surrounded by a perimeter fence of at least _____ feet high. (pages 98-99)

7. Which of the following are out of place in the safe jumping arena? (pages 98-99)

    a. standards with jackets hung on them   b. well-mannered dogs

    c. jump cups not in immediate use   d. rowdy dogs

    e. small children   f. all of the above

    g. none of the above

8. Before beginning the jumping part of the lesson, students should have spent _____ minutes doing their warm-up exercises and school figures for their horses. (page 99)

9. Why is "stopping on the line" important? (page 100)

10. Place the following items in an appropriate order to use as a checklist and cadence for jumping: squeeze eyes release heels straight. (page 100)

Control Issues:
Why Lesson Horses
Won't Stop

Sometimes beginners cannot stop their horses, even when their reins are short enough. The horse starts to trot fast. The beginner rider tries to pull back. Her feet are behind her. She pulls herself forward onto the neck. Her feet flail the flanks, and the horse begins to canter. Now the rider is bouncing wildly on top of the horse, which only urges him on. With luck, the horse is only a few steps from the others, because if he's not, the rider will fall off. She'll probably tumble off anyway, when the horse stops.

If the beginner rider's reins are too long when the horse begins to trot too fast, she will pull the reins back to her tummy, maybe up to her shoulders; the bouncing and flopping will begin, leading to the same result.

If the beginner has not been taught to bury her heels in an emergency, the feet will go back and all will be lost. **So build a base first and teach the emergency procedures in such a way that a beginner can use them.**

It is always better to learn the emergency procedures from a certified instructor or in a safety course rather than from a handbook. This handbook was designed to be used with a course of instruction, not by itself in place of instruction.

A. Emergency Dismount

If a rider knows he can get off more or less whenever he wants, he will have more confidence. That's why it's good to practice the emergency dismount. You don't want to have all your riders bail out at the canter all at once, but they can learn to get off either side at any gait. **You must be able to do this yourself if you are going to demonstrate it and teach it! You must do it first from both sides off any horse to be used for this purpose in a lesson.**

THE EMERGENCY DISMOUNT

The emergency dismount demonstrated at the canter. Riders should practice this maneuver from both sides of the horse. Note that the rider has landed away from the horse facing the same way that the horse is traveling, as she should.

All photos by Rick Raske

1.

At the command, "Prepare to bail," drop your stirrups; you are not yet committed. You can change your mind.

2.

At the command, "Bail out," lay the reins on the neck close to the ears and place your hands on the neck or pommel of the saddle.

3.

Swing one leg back and over . . .

4.

. . . while pushing up and away from the horse . . .

5.

. . . landing safely away from the horse, and facing the same direction that the horse is traveling.

Note: *Most horses will come to a complete standstill as soon as the rider shifts his weight to one side or the other, because they expect the rider to dismount. This is convenient for practice, but remember, a frightened horse will not stop.*

Start with the horse standing still, then:

Step 1: Drop your stirrups.

Step 2: Lay your reins up by the ears of the horse, or as far as you can reach, out of the way.

Step 3: Place your hands on the neck or saddle, whichever is more comfortable for you.

Step 4: Swing your legs forward and back as you lift on your hands and push off. You should be able to click your heels over the rump of the horse before you push off. One method of dismounting is to drop both stirrups and vault off. This is the same thing, with more enthusiasm.

The rider should land away from the horse facing the same way as the horse is traveling. If the horse is kicking up, better to be tagged in the back of your helmet than in the fall.

B. Emergency Stop

Many riders are afraid because they think they may not be able to stop the horse. Once they are taught and practice an emergency stop, they are no longer as fearful.

There are various ways to teach the emergency stop. This is the method we have developed in practice over several years. We have found that with ample practice, students respond quickly if a horse begins to take off, and that the runaway attempt is thwarted. In reality, most horses are not the blind, hysterical, creatures of the movies, but simple "Good Old Boys" headed home and do not develop into runaways.

Let's assume that the rider who needs the emergency stop is a novice with limited skills. The instructions, then, must be on a level that even the least accomplished rider can follow.

The horse may stop at any of the steps and probably will, so long as the rider keeps tension on the reins and his heels firmly down. The important things are to keep the tension on the reins all the time until the horse stops and to keep the heels down. **If the heels come up, the horse can pull the rider forward. When practicing the skill, use a very light touch. As always, it is best to learn this procedure from a certified instructor. Practice and then practice some more. Practice with a rope tied to a fence. Practice beginning with the right hand, too. Practice softly on the horse unless you have an emergency. (See p. 108).**

C. "My Horse Won't Turn!"

We all have experience with the lesson horse who insists on following his buddy or who edges back to the barn or to the middle of the arena next to the instructor. We watch the novice rider pull the head around, and the clever old horse just keeps going. Maybe the novice lets go and tries to turn him the other way. Then he lets go and goes back to the first direction. He tries and gives up and tries and gives up again. What's wrong? Why won't his horse turn?

THE EMERGENCY STOP

These photos show how to perform the emergency stop to the left. Practice, then practice some more, so that you can begin the sequence from either hand.

Start by putting your heels forward and placing both reins in one hand.

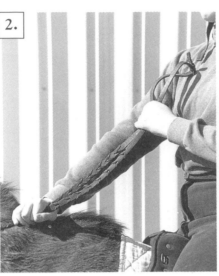

Grab the reins on the neck with the other hand, here the right, keeping tension on the reins at all times.

All photos by Dick Pond

Let go with your left hand and use it to grab only the left rein in front of your right hand. The right hand releases the left rein and begins pushing on the horse's neck.

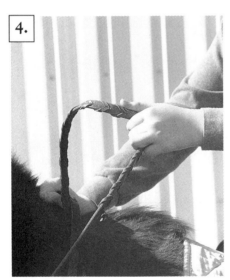

The right hand pushes on the neck while the left hand and rein pulls.

You're still pushing with the right hand, while your left hand pulls toward your left shoulder. Here, the rider has let her left rein slip a bit to avoid hurting the horse during the demonstration.

Don't let go, already!

Keep the horse's nose pointed where you want to go and **wait.** This bends the horse's body and makes him a bit uncomfortable. In a short while, the horse will straighten his body out, and you'll be headed in the right direction. After a couple of times, the average school horse will give the persistent novice respect and quit trying to go his own way.

This is a particularly valuable skill for a student to have if the horse is headed home (or anywhere the rider doesn't want to go) and especially if the horse is going too fast. In the effort to turn the resistant horse, the student may even have the horse's nose all the way to the rider's knee. He may have to pull the rein up as well as back. The point is to get the horse's head around as if to turn, then **wait.**

The horse will again straighten his body out. This is not a comfortable position for him. When he does straighten out, he will step across behind and be trotting — end of problem. This is called **doubling.** *Note:* Doubling is more difficult if the rider's lower legs are behind the vertical line formed by his correct alignment of ear, shoulder, hip, and heel.

D. The Importance of "Whoa"

Any horse can learn the word "whoa." It also sounds like "no," "go," "oh," even "oh! no!" To most horses, they are all the same. Tone of voice also is important. "Whoa" means stop, and when he does stop, the horse must be allowed to stand and rest a full minute or so. This becomes his motivation to respond to "Whoa." The horse should remain stopped until he exhales a large breath.

If you are consistent and always honor your "whoa" or something similar when said accidentally, your horse will always stop when he hears "whoa," especially when you need him to stop. Always say "whoa" in a soft firm voice that goes down the scale in tone.

Good Western riders usually already do this. Go to any reining horse competition, and there will always be several riders, sitting in the arena, on their horses, "doing nothing." This is called "dwell time." The horses are learning to whoa and stand quietly, even after spinning 360 degrees four times or doing a sliding stop of 30 feet or more.

"Whoa" is a good tool to have, as it allows the instructor to stop a horse when necessary. It's a good way to check a student's seat occasionally. If you can stop a lesson horse at will, you can show a student he is too far forward. "Whoa" also is a safety net, because a riding instructor, unlike the swimming instructor, cannot step or jump in and take control of a situation.

Unfortunately, the well-trained horse will whoa for just about anybody. Just like the old show horse who anticipates and follows the announcer's voice commands, a horse probably will whoa when any clown rides by and says "whoa" just right. Usually, however, the horse learns whose "whoa" counts. Protect your "whoa" by enforcing the stop and rest after the word.

1. Why can't beginners stop their horses? (page 105)

2. "Prepare to bail," means _____. (page 106)

3. Upon hearing "Bail out," the rider should _____. (page 106)

4. Where should the rider land after an emergency dismount? Which direction should she be facing? (page 106)

5. What are the five steps of the emergency stop? (page 108)

6. The horse may, and probably will, stop at any of the steps so long as the rider keeps _____ on the _____ and his/her _____ firmly down. (page 107)

7. "My horse won't turn." Why not? (pages 107 and 109)

8. When the horse hears "whoa," he must _____ completely and be allowed to _____ until he exhales. (page 109)

9. A good "whoa" is important to a riding instructor because when something goes wrong, she can _____ the horse. (page 109)

10. She can also use "whoa" to check a rider's _____ especially when the rider is convinced she is not leaning forward. (page 109)

THE SAFE SCHOOL HORSE

Good school horses usually are made after several years in a good school with a considerate instructor.

We all have our conceptions of the "ideal school horse." Maybe we even have been fortunate enough to own at least one horse that meets our "ideal" criteria. However, most of us also have financial restrictions to consider when we select school horses.

We must make decisions in selecting school, camp, or novice horses. This also includes most privately owned horses for beginners or young adults. What characteristics must we have? What can we live without if we must? How much training can we reasonably do after we acquire the new horse? If we are lucky enough to be allowed a trial period, given this extra time, what do we want to know about the horse in question?

The first consideration is the basic horse. Is he sound? Is he sane? Is he tolerant of mistakes? Is he the right age?

We say "he" — geldings are preferred by most, but some mares are suitable. Stallions are not suitable for beginners, novices, or young riders.

A. Age

The United States Pony Club requires that horses used in USPC competitions be at least 5 years old. At AAHS headquarters, we like to acquire school horses that are between 8 and 15 years old. Most are around 12 to 15. We have never accepted a school horse younger than 7. Some were in their 20s, but we knew those old-timers, and they were healthy and strong, sweet, and reliable.

B. Soundness — Physical and Mental

We excuse only a few soundness problems and then only on the advice of our veterinarians. One such horse had a slight heart murmur. The veterinarian said, "Don't race him." He proved to be an "ideal" school horse. It's hard to say exactly what will cause us to wash out a prospect. It is easier to give general guidelines of what we are looking for.

The horse must demonstrate true and correct rhythm in his gaits. He cannot be a "little off" or have an odd way of going that defies description even though he seems sound otherwise. Correct movement is a must. Some older horses may be slightly arthritic, but if they have correct gaits and are sound most of the time, they can usually carry walk-trot-level beginners on proper surfaces for several lessons a day. Requiring correct gaits eliminates about 25 percent of the horses that people offer free of charge or on permanent loan.

Any history of recurring illness, such as colic or founder, is cause for elimination. The economics of your program require this. Eliminate also for allergies or any other condition that requires constant medication or special treatment.

A horse that is recovering from a serious injury who "will probably be 100 percent" is not a good choice. If he's not sound after you have taken care of him, who will haul away the sweet old guy? We become attached to our horses quickly. Try not to become attached to ones who can't make a living. (We have a geriatrics pasture for those old-timers who have served us well. They have earned their retirement. We promised them they wouldn't be eaten, and we don't lie to our horses.)

Many school horses are donated by former boarders, so we know their history, and that helps. But if you have only 24 hours and an unknown horse, have the veterinarian check his heart, lungs, feet, eyesight, and hearing. You must get the stranger at a price that will let you move him in a few weeks if he won't work for you.

I see many school horses around the country — more than I would like — that are either not sound, or are sore, or get sore too quickly. This is not a good idea. It gives your program a bad image and certainly gives your students the wrong idea of horsemanship. The school horse is the backbone of any lesson program and should be treated like royalty. They are usually worth more to a program than an instructor.

Blemishes are OK; unsoundness is not. Our veterinarian helps us decide if a horse is sound for our purposes. We are not talking a big-ticket, prepurchase veterinarian examination, but simply a basic office exam for suitability. However, if you teach jumping, it's a good idea to have the veterinarian clear the horse for that specific purpose. We won't jump school horses over two feet six inches. After that, students need their own horses.

Many horses used as school horses for jumping have what is thought to be navicu-

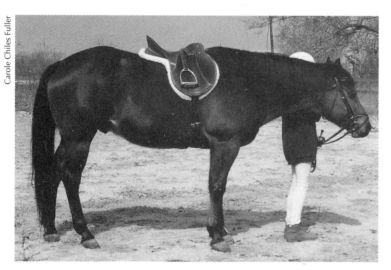

Carole Chiles Fuller

A good school horse must be calm and patient.

lar syndrome and have had some nerves surgically severed. Many veterinarians require the owner of the horse, at the time the procedure was done, to sign a waiver that he has been informed that the horse may no longer be safe to ride. You certainly don't want to lose a lawsuit because of an unsound horse that you should have known about. It's best to know what you buy, and know what not to use. What your veterinarian tells you is what he will have to swear he told you when he is under oath in court. Hear him the first time.

Mental soundness is next. The horse must be able to tolerate noise, flapping plastic, dogs, bicycles, wiggly riders, and little hands tacking up slowly and clumsily. A persnickety horse is not a good prospect, nor is one who is too flaky when handled from the ground.

C. Sanity or Sainthood

The school horse should be reliable and manageable in the lesson situation. At AAHS, we don't teach students how to ride on unruly horses.

The beginner horse should be as close to an equine saint as you can obtain. We can teach our beginners all the safety rules, but only time and correct, supervised practice will turn the rules into habits. In the meantime, kids occasionally will run or yell, horses may be tied improperly, bridles will not be put on with skill and ease. And the student hasn't even mounted yet!

The beginner school horse must have a high degree of tolerance. We must depend on these good souls not to react when something goes wrong. Even in the best barns, nothing is perfect. The best procedure in the world doesn't guarantee perfect performance from humans, so we look for horses who are habitually patient and kind.

They must like to be handled and not be too particular about how. If they are touchy or ticklish, simple grooming becomes a potential liability. If they are hard to catch, or require a ritual catching process, or must be caught with feed, they will waste time and may cause an accident.

Avoid horses that cannot be tied. I'm not kidding here. I have been to stables that had some school horses that could not be tied, so they stood free for grooming and tacking up. It's only a matter of time before a major distraction goes down the barn aisle and that untied horse is going to lose it. To say that he never has is not to say that he never will.

Avoid horses that are aggressively picky about their companions. They will make the lives of their corral mates miserable and your veterinarian bills higher.

Avoid horses that get weird or panicky in normal situations. Sometimes we discover this the hard way, but that is why the instructors, then the advanced students ride the newcomers for a while. All horses like to walk faster returning to the barn, be with their fellows, snort occasionally at the unusual sight or smell, and get frisky when the barometer falls or after a rain, but some horses carry this to dangerous extremes. Ride and handle the new school horse thoroughly yourself before a student ever rides it. It's best to keep him a staff horse for at least 30 days and then introduce him to advanced students, then intermediates, and lastly to beginners if he is finally deemed unanimously suitable.

D. Dangerous Vices

No school needs horses with known dangerous habits. What they do is your fault if you either know that they might do it or simply that they have done it once before. You will lose the lawsuit. One bucking spree, one bite, one kick, whether or not it caused an injury, and you should sell the horse unless you can absolutely identify the cause as something unique, such as a hot air balloon crash landing in the arena.

An instructor should not tolerate a particular vice because the horse is affordable. (These guidelines are just as valid for horses being sold to customers. You cannot afford to sell a horse with a dangerous vice even to an experienced rider with full disclosure — it can come back to haunt you.) Horses with dangerous vices go to the auction to sell "as is" with no accompanying history.

Dangerous Vices
- **Kicking** (at anything — humans, other horses, dogs, and so on). Do not accept this behavior from any school horse anywhere, ever. It is too great a liability. When a school horse kicks, he must go. You cannot afford to rationalize the behavior and give him a chance to kick again.
- **Biting.** Watch the ponies especially. Biters must go after the first bite. Ponies can sink their teeth into the little britches of a half-mounted rider and have him off in a heartbeat. Hand feeding can result in a vicious bite, so no hand feeding of the horses is permitted. It is just too easy for the sweet old horse to munch a little finger or two. He doesn't know until it's too late that a finger slipped into his mouth.
- **Striking.** This is aggression (as is biting). You can't afford it.
- **Crowding.** Some horses use crowding to avoid being saddled or handled. This is dangerous behavior that has no place in the school string.
- **Rearing.** If a horse rears while being led or while mounted, he absolutely cannot be in the school string. Not a good idea to sell out of your barn, either.
- **Bucking.** This is the difficult one. If a horse is left in the stall, hasn't been used, hasn't had his schedule varied, he may buck. If he bucks and tosses a rider, you must get rid of him because he has shown "dangerous propensities," that is, he bucks, and you know it. So don't let your lack of consideration for the needs of your school horses result in a behavior that will force you to get rid of a good horse. Don't set a horse up to buck! When in doubt, turn him out or, at the very least, longe him.
- **Sitting or pulling back.** The horse can fall or the suddenness can capture fingers in a rope and sever them.

E. Lesson Horses That Schools Don't Need

The problems in this list may not qualify as dangerous vices, but they should disqualify horses from your school string.

Disqualifying Vices

- **Mares that have difficult heat periods.** This is particularly important in the southern United States, where mares may be in transitional estrous several months. This can be chronic premenstrual syndrome (PMS).

- **Shying.** You may make an exception for bad behavior that results from something obvious, such as a bee sting, over which you have no control; but make no exceptions for shying at bicycles, blowing plastic, other horses playing, and other normal distractions. Your school horses must ignore all of these.

- **The runaway.** He starts as a horse who likes to follow too closely or catch up too quickly and ends up as the horse tearing around the ring — it may only be at the trot, but he won't stop. You don't need him. Don't buy him. Don't help make a runaway, either. Adhere strictly to spacing rules in the ring and on the trail. Watch for warning signs. After one inexplicable runaway, the horse must go.

- **Barn sour.** This is the horse who doesn't like to leave the barn. Little by little, he will try harder and harder to stay put. Soon, he may be standing on his hind legs and going over backward with your customer or student. Don't buy him, thinking that you will cure him. He'll just wait for another opportunity. Follow the rule "walk the last mile home"; vary your rides so horses don't associate one spot with a turn toward home.

- **Hurries to catch up.** All horses like to be with their buddies; not all horses insist on it. Get rid of one who does. There are many horses who will walk and trot happily at a safe distance from other horses.

- **Head rubbers.** They want to scratch. They must learn to wait until the bridle and halter are off. They can catch their bridle or halter on something and panic, knock a child over or underfoot, or push a person down or in front of a vehicle. We have a rule: People may touch the horses; the horses may not touch the people. If rubbing behavior is not successfully overcome, get rid of the horse.

- **Bucks after a jump.** Not good. Novices fall off. Every horse may do this once in a while if not warmed up properly, but the horse who does it because the rider was off balance, got left behind, or hit the horse in the mouth shouldn't be in the lesson string because novices may do these things while learning to jump. Be sure to get all horses warmed up properly or you will be having to get rid of a "bucker" because he has a history, when in fact it was an instructor's error.

- **Runs out or stops while jumping.** Too difficult for novices. School horses must be reliable. Running out or stopping may cause a fall. All horses will do this occasionally; we are talking now about the horse who does this on a routine basis. You don't want a child on the witness stand saying, "He always ran out." Kids tend to exaggerate so it is better to exercise extreme caution. Don't push your students too fast into jumping or they will mess up your reliable horses.

Ross Chapple

Cribbers might make acceptable school horses if they don't have to be stalled much and don't crib while they are in the pasture.

F. Stable Vices

In the school string, we try to avoid horses with stable vices, but these are not the same hard-and-fast rules that must apply to horses with dangerous vices.

If a cribbing or wind-sucking horse doesn't indulge in this behavior when turned out, we'll take him and not stall him. We have one cribber in the barn who wears a cribbing collar at night in the barn and is fine when he's turned out all day. When he's brought into the stall, he won't play with toys, but he will twirl his cribbing collar when it comes off, which seems to keep him happy.

Stall-weaving is not a problem in a school horse if the school horses are turned out or are in large corrals. No stall, no stall-weaver. If such a horse must be kept in a stall, it may be best to pass him up, because there is evidence that other horses may copy these self-stimulation habits.

G. Behavior Under Saddle

A horse who has had serious behavior problems in the past is not a good candidate for a lesson horse. Even if he has been "straightened out," he may well revert to early behaviors as soon as he figures out that there is a student in the saddle. The difficulty with horses with behavior problems as lesson horses is that each time the behavior succeeds or the student gives up, the horse is rewarded for the bad behavior. Remember, the horse cannot connect a behavior and a consequence that are more than a few seconds apart. There isn't time in many cases for the instructor to get on and fix a problem. A student is often not capable of handling the problem horse's evasions. Over time, the evasions get bigger and usually more dangerous, which require skill that the average student doesn't have.

H. How to Find Problems Safely

Ask. Ask specifically. Have a list. "Does this horse ever . . .?" Then go down the list. If the veterinarian says he is sound enough for the purpose you want and he seems tolerant and kind, try him out. Even if he seems wonderful, don't take him for granted when you get him home. Good, inexpensive horses are scarce. Most have some problems. If they didn't the horse would have passed to another owner without being offered to you. Be wary of gift horses unless they come from your own students and you know the horse. You must do your best to spot the problems and avoid them before they cause an accident. Some problems you can live with and some you cannot.

I know of one school horse at a stable who is used to teach jumping. He would carry novices all day in the ring and cross country over obstacles up to two feet six inches. At three feet, no force on earth could hold him, so he wasn't asked to jump that high with less experienced riders. This was a judgment call that never caused the stable any trouble. I would not have accepted this horse.

A safe instructor should ride every horse she will use in a lesson and in every situation in which a lesson will be taught — before the lesson is taught. An instructor should never use a horse she cannot ride comfortably. You cannot teach someone to do something you can't do. In addition, there should be a procedure for trying potential lesson horses before they actually are used in a real lesson with a student aboard.

The procedure we recommend involves testing the horse's capacity for tolerance and temptation within reason. The horse should be handled in the barn correctly and observed carefully. The instructor should already know if he is easy to catch, tack up, and ride. Next, it is necessary to see how the horse behaves in company and especially by himself. Although we try never to have anyone alone on a horse, sometimes the horse perceives himself to be alone or about to be left behind. (On a cross-country course or in a Western trail class, the horse perceives himself to be alone.) We need to know how he will act in the arena or on the trail when this happens.

The easiest thing to do is ride the horse in the company of two or three other instructors or experienced staff. See how the horse behaves if they are trotting or cantering and you are not, and vice versa. Can you safely ride this horse in one part of the arena when the others are in another part? Can you mount and dismount safely in the arena? Is he easy to slow down and stop? It is better to have to push a lesson horse than to have difficulty stopping one.

If the horse is to be used on the trail, will he behave if the others go out of sight around a corner? Sometimes students don't keep up. If something spooks the others, does he automatically spook also? If the other horses become fractious, will he remain quiet? If you dismount to open and close a gate, will he calmly allow you to do so? Can he tolerate the tractor? The golf cart? Many horses do not care for electric golf carts, and some never get used to them. (A new employee may not know the horse or remember.)

You would never allow your students to ride away from the group, but what happens if one of them does? Kids and adults equally are likely to stretch your rules. You may not be responsible if specific rules are deliberately broken, but you still don't want an accident. Thus, you need to know about your lesson horses, camp horses, and trail horses even in prohibited situations. This does not mean you should take unnecessary risks in finding out this information. Within reason, however, you need to make sure the horse does not change character suddenly under certain circumstances.

You can ride with another experienced staff member and check out how this horse will behave if he thinks he is separated from his buddies or the barn. You can carefully test how he will behave if his companion turns for home and he is asked to proceed. Ask the other staff member to trot or canter on a short way ahead so you can see whether the new horse will keep walking quietly or appears to be willing to do so with a little practice.

All of these field tests involve situations that are common. We may not want them to happen, but they will, and even when they don't, the horse may perceive the situation differently. Check out each horse gradually and carefully. Don't try to rationalize because he's cheap, because he seems gentle, or because he belonged to a beloved customer who wants to give him to you. Don't take any chances with your own safety. If you are uncomfortable with the new horse at any time, there probably is a reason.

Having an accident usually means that someone made a mistake. Don't let that person be you.

Several years ago an instructor of Western riding was offered a retired reining horse for her camp program. She knew the horse and the owner and accepted gratefully. The horse worked well in the lesson ring, but an accident occurred before the instructor realized that she had no idea of the horse's experience on the trail. The horse had none. He thought nature was pretty scary. No matter how wonderful the prospective horse is, **try him in all the situations in which he is to be used; you may avert an accident.** The reiner could have been educated to the trail, and the accident would not have happened.

I. If the Lesson Horse Is a Mare

Don't take anyone's word for how a mare will act during her heat cycle or during transitional estrous when cycling begins in the spring or ends in the fall. Mares can and often do have PMS.

The instructor must know her mares. View mares as you would a teenager, because they are under tremendous hormonal pressure at various times throughout the year.

J. The Sour School Horse

Lots of different opinions exist about the sour school horse and how to rehabilitate him and make him feel better. But we all understand that the sour school horse is at best a problem and at worst a liability.

A comfortable horse is a safe horse. An uncomfortable horse is a dangerous horse. School horses become sour because they become uncomfortable for a variety of reasons.

Keep Lesson Horses Comfortable

Too heavy a lesson schedule will sour a school horse; so will mismatching students and horses. The more sensitive horses are not good candidates for beginners because beginners move around too much, and sensitive horses don't have that much tolerance. Tolerance is what you are born with; patience is what you are taught.

Boring lessons also will sour a school horse. If the instructor is bored or boring, chances are the students and horses are bored as well. Bored students and horses are at risk. Horses and students need a change of pace. This means different activities and games. Variety can be achieved safely in the ring. The instructor must exercise her imagination. Fight school-horse burnout. (Variety will help prevent instructor burnout, too, which may be even more dangerous.)

Too many longe lessons or too many beginners and not enough advanced riders will cause a school horse to shut down and stop responding. We start pounding and demanding more, and then we have a more serious problem.

In a show barn, a steady diet of lessons and shows with no break can seriously affect the morale of school and show horses alike. They become stressed just as we do. A change in the program or rotated rest and relaxation periods will help.

Horses need at least one day off each week. They also need a limit to the number of hours they work each day, with sufficient breaks during which they can be unsaddled and have a rest.

A fair schedule is four hours of lessons a day or six trail ride hours, depending on the terrain. Also, keep the following in mind:

- Limit jumping lessons to two each day — if more, limit the amount of jumping in each lesson.
- Six arena hours a day should be the absolute tops.
- Three lessons of no more than 40 minutes with breaks during and between each lesson is the limit of longe lessons for longe horses.

We also try to give each horse a 30-day vacation at least once a year — more for one who is used heavily or whose work is especially stressful. If you are fortunate enough to be located where you have access to grassy pastures and can turn out your horses, there will be considerably fewer problems with burnout. A dry lot doesn't work as well, but if your horses are out together with fresh grass hay and clean water, that will help.

It is important to keep track of each horse's work schedule so they all get the rest and variety they need. After all, the horses carry the weight and are the mainstay of any lesson program.

The best cure for sour school horses is not to make them sour in the first place. Their tack should be comfortable. They should be kept clean. They should live in a clean place with good grain, hay, and fresh water. They should have regular exercise besides lessons, if possible. They should have time off — at least one day a week and one month a year. Their mental health is important, and it is their mental health that is not good when they are "sour." Most importantly, the instructor must insist that they are ridden correctly and should not ask wobbly hands to ride with contact. Instructors should keep lessons well within the rider's level of competence so that students can follow directions smoothly. If you don't, you'll just have bouncing bodies, jerky hands, and bumping legs on the riders of most your school horses.

K. Special Training for the School Horse

When you acquire a school horse, he may not have all the training you will need. He should perform fairly willingly when asked correctly. He should be easy to ride. He need not be perfect.

It may be necessary to improve his taking a particular lead. You may have to teach him a leg yield or basic jumping or Western maneuvers. He must respond to the word "whoa" when it is uttered by someone other than his rider. You also may want to teach him voice commands.

The point is that it is OK to train the horse in basic skills. It is not OK to attempt to train a school horse out of bad behavior. Even if you succeed, he still has a bad history, and a bad history is a serious liability for a school horse or one purchased for a minor or a novice if the horse for any reason reverts to his previous behavior.

L. The Former Racehorse

Former racehorses (the slow ones) often make excellent hunters and jumpers. However, they are not good candidates for school horses. If such a horse runs off and injures a student, you will find yourself in a position that's difficult to defend. Saying, "Gee, he never did that before!" doesn't help if he has been to the track or fully in race training.

Chapter 13 — Review Questions

1. Select the characteristics that are desirable in a school horse: (pages 111-118)

    a. only slightly gimpy   b. completely sane

    c. hasn't bucked off a rider in six months d. three years old

    e. good teeth   f. twelve years old

    g. a mare constantly in season   h. gelding who forgives everything

2. Boomer is a popular school horse. He does freak out when the UPS truck comes, but only if it comes early in the morning. Should we keep him as a school horse? (page 113)

3. Name five dangerous vices. (page 114)

4. If a cribber or stall-weaver must be stalled, then we will/will not buy him as a school horse. (page 116)

5. List three bad behaviors of lesson horses that schools don't needs other than bucking, kicking, and running away. (pages 114-115)

6. We are one horse short for the 10 a.m. class. Can we use Pepper even though he arrived just yesterday? Ms. Weyland rode her yesterday and said she was fine. (page 117)

7. What is an easy way to safely test a potential school horse on the trail? In the arena? (page 117)

8. Should you try this horse alone even though students are not allowed to ride alone? How can you do this safely? (page 117)

9. How do you avoid having a sour school horse in your string? (pages 118-119)

10. When the ex-racehorse (now school horse) runs away and causes an injury, is the "Gee, he never did that before" defense a good one? (page 120)

Appendix A

DEALING WITH ACCIDENTS AND LAWSUITS

Robert O. Dawson
Bryant Smith Chair in Law, University of Texas School of Law
J.D., Washington University School of Law, 1963
S.J.D., University of Wisconsin School of Law, 1969

Most of this handbook is about how to have an effective teaching program that also is safe. The emphasis is upon how to avoid having accidents. If steps are taken by the instructor that prevent only one serious accident, they will have been well worth their cost and trouble. A major accident, even if the student fully recovers with minimal pain and suffering, deals a blow to the safety reputation of the stable and lesson program. It certainly will adversely affect staff and student morale. It also is very likely to affect business.

When a lawsuit is added to the consequences of an accident, the adverse impact on the business and the people involved becomes multiplied many times.

This chapter begins with what to do when there is an accident from a legal point of view. It next discusses the release-from-liability form that most riding stables require prospective students to sign. Then it discusses the special problems of minor children who are riding students, then liability insurance and what it does and doesn't do to protect the instructor. And last, it deals with what to do when you receive notification that a lawsuit has been filed against you.

What to Do When There Is an Accident

When there is an accident, the first steps you need to take are:
1. Secure the area so that further accidents are not caused by panicked horses or students. Advanced students or other staff, if present, can do this while you concentrate on the injured student. However, they must have been previously trained in emergency procedures to do this for you, and those procedures should be in the staff manual.

2. Examine the injured student in an effort to determine the nature and extent of the injuries. Do not move the injured student until the nature and extent of the injuries have been determined because moving her may aggravate those injuries. Current, certified first-aid and CPR training are essential to making this preliminary evaluation correctly. If possible, all staff should have this training.

3. Have someone call the emergency medical service if that seems required from your preliminary evaluation. Your stables should already have posted by each telephone the EMS phone number and directions to give to EMS so they can locate your stable promptly. Many rural areas have been assigned physical addresses specifically for EMS, so you will need to find out about your own area before you need emergency services. Check out your 911 service in advance, as it is not unheard of that your 911 service is connected to the wrong EMS unit. This is especially likely if you live close to a county line or city limit.

4. Take the necessary steps of first aid or of CPR while awaiting the arrival of the EMS. Use the first-aid kit that is available in the barn or that the instructor brought on the trail ride. It is essential that the instructor is certified in both first-aid and CPR. Without that training, more harm than good can be done by administering first aid beyond the obvious step of attempting to stop any bleeding. Let EMS personnel remove a helmet if the injured person cannot. You may unhook the chin strap.

5. Have someone notify parents or other relatives of the injured student. It may become important that those persons be consulted by medical staff concerning various courses of treatment.

6. If the injured student is a minor child, have someone get the book in which Medical Consents are filed. Give the student's Medical Consent form to the EMS driver or take it with you to the emergency room or clinic if you are transporting the injured student. (Medical consents are discussed later in this chapter.)

Your Attitude Toward the Accident

Your attitude toward the injured student and the accident is very important. The first priority is to obtain prompt and appropriate medical attention for the student and to ensure that the accident does not result in further accidents involving other horses and students. In an ideal world, that would be the instructor's only concern. But in the real world, the instructor must also be concerned about a possible lawsuit. Remember the following:

1. What you say about the accident is extremely important. You cannot avoid talking about the accident to EMS personnel, medical personnel in the emergency room or clinic, parents, other students or customers, an employer, and other instructors.

2. While you cannot avoid talking about the accident and how it happened, you must avoid assuming fault yourself or attempting to assign it to others, such as the injured student, other students, observers, or the horse. You must describe the accident and how it happened. **You must not attempt to assign a cause for the accident because that inevitably leads to the question of fault.** You can describe an accident fully and accurately **without trying to describe why you think the accident occurred.**

3. There is a strong desire on the part of compassionate people to want to assume fault for an accident in which they have been involved. You may feel better saying to a parent, "My goodness, I'm so sorry this happened to your child; it's all my fault. I should have. . . ." Unfortunately, when you examine the accident calmly later, you may conclude it wasn't really your fault after all, or only partially your fault, but the damage will have been done. If there is a lawsuit, your initial statement, made in the stress of the moment, almost certainly will come back to haunt you. It will be used against you in the lawsuit.

4. It is also important that you talk about the accident only to certain people. You may safely talk about the accident to your spouse because confidential communications to a spouse are legally privileged and cannot be compelled to be divulged. You may also freely talk about the accident to an attorney who is or may be representing you concerning the accident. Those communications are also confidential and may not be compelled to be divulged. In fact, you *should* talk freely and candidly to your attorney, because he or she cannot effectively represent you without such information.

You will also have to talk with your employer about the accident, even though that information may not be a privileged communication. A formal written report to your employer should be made promptly. Again, it is very important that the report state only the facts and not attempt to determine the cause of the accident or to assume or assign fault.

The Release from Liability

Almost all riding stables have a prospective student sign a *release-from-liability* form before they permit the student to mount a horse. Some of these forms protect the stables from lawsuit in the event of an accident. Others do not. Whether you have an effective release form depends upon (1) the state in which your stable is located and (2) the exact wording of the form. You cannot control where you are doing business, but you can control what the form says, because it's your form.

Negligence

As a general matter, the consequences of an accident fall upon the person injured. Just because a student or rider was injured at your stable does not mean that you are liable for the injury. If the injury was the fault of the person injured or was nobody's fault, then the injured person must suffer the burden alone.

If the injury was the fault of the horse, then the injured person must suffer the burden alone, unless you were at fault as trainer or caretaker of the horse or at fault in matching up the rider with the horse.

However, if the injury was wholly or partly your fault — perhaps by using unsafe teaching procedures, or by teaching a lesson in an unsafe environment, or by using a lesson horse that you knew had unsafe habits — then the injured person may believe that misery loves company and decide to sue you, the stables, and the insurer for money to compensate for the injuries. That is where your "release from liability" comes into play.

Almost always, the fault that is claimed to have caused the injury is *negligence*. Negligence means carelessness, but only carelessness of a type that a reasonable member of your profession (riding instructor) would not have permitted.

If the carelessness is particularly severe, it may be called *gross negligence* or *willful negligence*. At best, a release from liability can prevent a successful lawsuit for ordinary negligence; but even a perfect release-from-liability form cannot, in most states, protect you from a lawsuit for gross or willful negligence.

Are Releases Valid?

Almost all courts take the position that releases from liability "are not favored and must be strictly construed against the benefiting party, particularly one who drafted the release" (*Harris v. Walker*, 519 N.E.2d 917 [Ill. 1988]). This means that if the language of the release is at all vague, it will be interpreted in favor of the injured person. It is imperative, therefore, that the language employed in a release from liability be precise.

In some states, such as New York, releases for recreational activities have been invalidated because of a statute enacted by legislators that simply declares releases from liability invalid when a customer pays a fee to enter onto the land of another for recreation. This statute has been applied to riding stables and invalidates releases signed by riders (*Brancati v. Bar-U-Farm, Inc.*, 583 N.Y.S.2d 660 [App. Div. 1992]).

What the Release Should Say

Some release-from-liability forms try to do too much and, therefore, encounter strong resistance from courts that are asked to enforce them. For example, one release form stated that the riding student agreed "to assume full responsibility and liability for any and all personal injury associated with the riding of any horse or horses" at the stable. When that language was raised in defense to a lawsuit, the court stated that the release "purports to cause [the rider] to assume full responsibility for anything that may happen to [the rider] or anyone else while riding. It purports to provide such comfort for everyone in the world. Such a clause is so general as to be meaningless" (*Tanker v. North Crest Equestrian Center*, 621 N.E.2d 589 [Ohio App. 1993]).

It is important that the form release the stable, owners, and employees from liability for ordinary negligence in the operation of the stable. It also should specifically exclude releasing from liability for gross or willful negligence, so as not to appear overbroad and encounter a court's resistance for that reason. For instance, the language recommended by the North American Horsemen's Association is excellent. It releases the stable from liability "due to this stable's ordinary negligence" and states: ". . . except in the event of this stable's gross and willful negligence, I shall bring no claims, demands, actions and causes of action, and/or litigation, against this stable for any economic and non economic losses due to bodily injury, death, property damage, sustained by me and/or my minor child or legal ward in relation to the premises and operations of this stable, [including] while riding, handling, or otherwise being near horses owned by or in the care, custody, and control of this stable."

Having the Student Sign the Release

It is crucial that the rider or parent read the release from liability before signing it. Therefore, it should be signed in the presence of an employee of the stable. That employee would be available to answer any questions the prospective student has about the form before signing it and could if necessary testify that the rider read the release before signing it.

Further, it is important that no employee of the stable should in any way downplay the importance of the release. Statements such as, "This is just a formality," "This doesn't mean anything," and "This is just for my insurance company" will come back to haunt the stable in the event of an accident with injuries and a lawsuit. Those and similar statements permit the injured person to claim that he was misled as to what he was signing and therefore cannot be held to it.

Warnings That Accompany Releases

Releases from liability are usually accompanied by warnings about how a person can become injured when on or near a horse. These warnings are just as important as the release from liability and in some states — where releases from liability are invalid or at best shaky — they are more important. Consider the following:

1. The release from liability can operate only as to risks that are in some sense known by the person signing the release. The warnings prove that the person signing the release was aware of those risks because they were explained in black and white.

2. Even if releases from liability are invalid in your state in some or all situations, you can sometimes show that the rider by his or her own conduct has assumed the risk of such an accident occurring if you can prove the rider was informed of typical horse hazards and chose nevertheless to ride at your stable.

3. Those warnings may become important in assessing to what extent, if any, the injured person was in part at fault in the accident. If a riding hazard is explained in a warning and the rider nevertheless engaged in the warned-against conduct, then a good case can be made that he was at fault in the accident. In many states, if the injured person was more at fault than the stable, the stable wins.

4. Even if the judge or jury concludes that the stable was more at fault than the rider, the amount of the money awarded as damages is reduced in accordance with the assessment of fault. Thus, if the damages were assessed at $100,000 and the judge or jury found that the rider had 40 percent of the fault and the stable 60 percent, the stable and/or insurer would be required to pay $60,000 instead of $100,000.

Stressing the Written Warnings

The written warnings are so important that they should be stressed to the prospective student. They should be read and signed in the presence of an employee of the stable. In addition, the prospective student, *and* his parent if the student is a minor, should be required to write out in his own hand a statement that he has read and understood the warnings.

Safety Emphasis during Lessons

Further, the initial lesson should focus on educating the rider on safety hazards and procedures. Stress on safety throughout the lesson program is important to the prevention of accidents. When an accident occurs, your stress on safety can also be your best defense to a lawsuit.

When the Injured Student Is a Minor Child

If you're in the horse business, you're probably also in the kid business. A child (minor) is a person under the age of 18. Children occupy a special place in the eyes of the law.

"Contracts" with a Child

A child cannot enter into a legally binding contract for the purchase of goods or services unless the goods or services are regarded as *necessaries*. Horses, horse boarding, horse renting, and riding lessons are not necessaries in the eyes of the law.

For this reason, a release signed by a minor child is not binding on the child. It is voidable and the child can disavow it simply by bringing a lawsuit after being injured. In other words, it is not worth the paper it is written on as a release. (*Smoky v. McCray*, 396 S.E.2d 794 [Ga. App. 1990], release signed by a 14-year-old is not valid as a release.)

However, just because the release is not valid as a release does not mean that you shouldn't use one when dealing with a child. The warnings about the nature of the horse and the risks of horseback riding that ordinarily accompany the release can become important even when the student is a child. A child who is at least 7 years of age is capable of being negligent. Therefore, if he is injured in an accident that was partially his fault (considering his age and experience with horses), he may not be able to sue successfully or, at least, the award may be reduced by the extent of his negligence compared to that of the stables. (*Willenbring v. Borkenhagen*, 139 N.W.2d 53 [Wis. 1966], 17-year-old was 40 percent negligent in a trail ride accident.)

Therefore, it is important that an employee explain to the child in language that the child can understand the nature of horses and the risks of handling and riding them. The child's signature on the release may not operate to excuse the stables, but it would still be evidence that the child read and had the warnings explained to him. That would, in turn, be important in assessing the child's negligence or assumption of risk by conduct.

Dealing with Parents

Every injury to a minor child creates at least three possible claims: (1) by the child for the injuries, (2) by the child's mother for loss of the child's services and for reimbursement of medical expenditures made by the mother on behalf of the child, and (3) by the child's father for loss of services and medical expense reimbursement.

A release signed by a mother or father prevents only the person who signed the release from suing for injuries to the child, and may not prevent the child or other parent from suing for those injuries. (*Rogers v. Donelson-Hermitage Chamber of Commerce*, 807 S.W.2d 242 [Tenn. App. 1990], release signed by the mother did not prevent the father from suing for the death of his minor child.)

A release signed by the minor child, her mother, and her father will at most prevent a successful lawsuit by the mother and father, but probably will not prevent the child's suit for his or her own injuries. Nothing can prevent that because the child cannot sign a binding agreement not to sue and parents probably cannot sign away the child's rights.

Nevertheless, the warnings that accompany the release are important even when the riding student is a minor child, and it is important that those warnings be given to a parent as well as the child. While it is unlikely that a release under those circumstances will prevent a lawsuit, the warnings will become significant in assessing fault for the accident should a lawsuit be filed. (*Bulkin v. Camp Nockamixon*, 79 A.2d 234 [Penn. 1951], permitting a 10-year-old camper to ride over his mother's expressed disapproval was negligence.)

Getting Medical Treatment for Injuries

If a minor child is injured in a horse accident while at your stable, you will want to obtain effective emergency medical attention. Whether you present the child to an emergency room or call an ambulance to transport the child, the hospital will have two concerns: (1) consent to treatment and (2) financial responsibility.

Without consent of a parent or guardian, many medical procedures that might be employed in the emergency treatment of a minor child for a horse-related accident would be batteries and grounds for a lawsuit. The child is incapable legally of giving effective consent to the medical procedures. In the eyes of the law, the procedures are conducted without consent and are, therefore, batteries.

Also, while a child might be able to enter into a binding contract for medical attention that legally is a "necessary," most hospitals would be reluctant to enter into such a contract with a minor without evidence of her ability to pay. In short, the hospital wants evidence of health insurance before it treats the child.

Medical Consent Form

Both parental consent to treatment and evidence of insurance can be put into the same form. Once the form is signed and notarized (see p. 128), it should be placed in a three-hole binder with other medical consent forms. If a child is injured, one has only to grab the entire binder in the emergency of the moment; there is no need to look through individual files for the particular consent form for the injured child.

The following form would be legally sufficient in most states.

The form should be signed in the presence of an employee who is a notary public and who witnesses the signature by signing the form and affixing the notary seal to it. In most states, becoming a notary is easy and inexpensive, so there is no reason why each stable can't have at least one on the premises.

In addition to the important purpose of identifying insurance information and persons to notify, having the parent fill out that information is powerful evidence that the form was read before it was signed.

Insurance: What It Does and Doesn't Do

Most riding teachers have insurance to cover their instruction or are employees of stables that have insurance to cover them.

Independent Contractor versus Employee

Unfortunately, some stables seek to avoid the expense of providing insurance for instructors by attempting to make the instructors *independent contractors* rather than

Consent to Emergency Medical, Dental, or Surgical Treatment for Minor Child

My name is _____. I am the (mother) (father) (guardian) of _____, a minor child and a riding student at _____.

I hereby consent to any medical, dental, or surgical treatment or procedure of an emergency nature that is reasonably necessary to save the life of the minor child named above or to restore the child to health.

Name of Insurance Company_____Policy Number_____

I understand that should medical emergency treatment be required, the current insurance information listed here will be provided to the attending clinic or hospital to cover future payment of incurred bills.

Emergency Phone Numbers:

Number	Person to Contact	Number	Person to Contact
_____	_____	_____	_____
_____	_____	_____	_____

(signed) _____ (date)_____

SWORN TO AND SUBSCRIBED before me this ___ day of _____, in the year _____.

_____Notary Public in and for the State of _____.

My Commission Expires:_____.

---

employees. If the riding instructor is an employee of the stable, then the stable is liable, along with the instructor, for any injury to a student that is the fault of the instructor.

However, if the riding instructor is truly an independent contractor, then the stable is not liable for an injury to a student due exclusively to the fault of the instructor. Just calling an instructor an independent contractor does not make her one. When all the dust settles, a court will look at several factors in addition to what the instructor and stable have called the relationship to decide whether the instructor was an independent contractor or an employee.

Some of the factors are whether the instructor teaches for only one stable or more than one, whether the instructor uses her own equipment and horses in teaching the lessons or those of the stable, whether the instructor is paid directly by the student and remits part to the stable as "rent" or whether the stable collects the fee and pays the instructor a part, and whether the stable controls or has the right to control any of the details of how the instructor does her job while on the premises. If the instructor teaches at more than one stable, uses her own equipment and horses, receives payment directly, and is not controlled by the stables as to how she teaches, the relationship begins to look like an independent contractor relationship. To the extent that those factors are not present, the relationship looks more like an employee relationship.

If the contract between the instructor and the stable characterizes the relationship as being one of an independent contractor, that may be a clue that the stable either does not have insurance or has insurance that protects only the stable and not also the instructor. Either possibility should be of grave concern to the instructor.

What Insurance Does

Liability insurance does two things for the person covered: First, up to the amount of the policy limits, it pays any judgment that may be obtained against the insured person for an activity covered by the policy. Second, it provides an attorney to defend a lawsuit against an insured for a covered activity. The insurance company selects and pays the attorney, but the attorney is representing the injured person as well as the company.

Some instructors may have the attitude, "I'm covered by insurance, so I don't have to worry about an accident." That's a big mistake.

First, some insurance policies have important exclusions from coverage. They may cover accidents only if they occur on the premises of the stable, and exclude accidents that may occur at a show, or while hauling, or on a trail ride off the premises. If that happens, you are not insured.

Second, if you are covered, you are covered only up to the policy limits. If the insurance policy has a $100,000 limit, for example, but a judgment of $200,000 is obtained, you and your employer are each personally liable for the additional $100,000. If the accident resulted in serious injuries with extensive medical treatment or has permanent consequences, it is easy for a judgment to exceed typical policy limits.

Third, some policies contain rather large deductibles, so you may have to pay several hundred or even several thousand dollars of the judgment even if it is covered by insurance.

The "I'm-Judgment-Proof" Fallacy

There also may be an attitude exhibited by riding instructors who because of youth or otherwise do not have many assets that, "What, me worry? You can't get blood out of a turnip. Let them sue, I'm judgment-proof." It may be that you are judgment-proof now because the only assets you possess are, in your state, exempt from seizure in satisfaction of judgments. However, you probably do not plan to remain in that condition for the rest of your life. Judgments can be renewed periodically so that they can be collected on indefinitely.

Thus, if you later inherit some wealth, or acquire a significant savings from your work, or discover oil on the back forty, you may find the judgment from your past rearing its ugly head to seize some of your assets. Also, the existence of an unpaid judgment on file against you is detrimental to your personal credit rating and business reputation.

What to Do If You Are Sued

A lawsuit can be filed against you for an accident anytime before the applicable *statute of limitations* expires. This will ordinarily be at least two years after the accident and can, under some circumstances, be significantly longer. The statute of limitations may be written in terms of when the person "knew or should have known" about the injury. Some injuries do not become apparent until years later, especially some back injuries.

How You Know You Are Being Sued

The first indication that you are going to be sued may come in the form of a "demand letter" from an attorney. This is likely to be somewhat nasty in its tone and to demand immediate payment of a large amount of money or a lawsuit will be filed. Do not respond to that letter.

Another, more direct, way in which you will learn about the lawsuit occurs when a deputy sheriff or constable serves you with the papers in the case. In some states, you may receive a certified letter, return receipt requested, containing the papers in the case. Don't worry, you won't be arrested and taken to jail.

Immediately Contact a Lawyer

Either way, contact your insurance company if you have not already done so. If you, or your employer, are not insured, contact a lawyer as soon as possible. While lawyers' services tend to be expensive, a brief, initial consultation to assess your situation can usually be arranged for a reasonable fee. It is clearly worth that fee, in peace of mind if for no other reason, to have that initial consultation.

It is very important that you not attempt personally to deal with the lawyer for the injured student. If you attempt to do so, you will almost certainly do yourself legal damage. Get your own lawyer and let him have all contact with the other side. That's what you're paying him for, and that's what he's trained to do.

It is also very important that you do not talk about the case with anyone except your own lawyer. Remember, anything you say can be used against you in a court of law.

Cooperate with Your Lawyer

From that point on, do what your lawyer tells you to do. He's the expert. Be completely candid with him. Your lawyer cannot effectively represent you unless you have told the whole truth, the bad as well as the good. Being sued is never pleasant, but it can be survived with body, soul, and assets intact.

Appendix B

SAMPLE STAFF MANUAL

Brenda Tallmon
B.A., equine management, Doane College, 1987
Stable manager, instructor, and head of horseback riding program,
at Lutherlyn Stables, a 22-horse, year-round program in Butler, Pennsylvania
AAHS safety-certified riding instructor

This manual is intended to be used as a guideline for stable owners and managers. It is designed to help the individual horse operation compile its own staff guidelines. It should contain everything you want your staff (instructors, grooms, office personnel, and so on) to know.

To add or subtract various sections, to tailor the manual to staff members, we suggest a loose-leaf book form, and possibly color coding the different sections for easier accessibility. These guidelines may also be rearranged in any order to fit your barn or staff priorities.

Examples in this manual are only a few of what should be a well-thought-out, thorough list of policies and procedures. A finished manual will be quite extensive. All examples in this sample manual are to be used to enable you to think of what rules and policies you need to set for your own staff to follow.

Everything that the staff will be held responsible for on a regular basis must be in your staff manual. The manual is your proof that you have these procedures in place and that your staff has been informed of them. This can be very important should an accident occur and a lawsuit be filed against you.

For more specific ideas of what can actually be included in your own manual, you may refer back to Chapters 1 through 3.

A. Guidelines for Instructors

1. Safety rules: What are they? Examples:
- Safety of people and horses is the number one priority at all times.
- Safety regulations must be thoroughly explained personally and followed at all times by everybody.

- Think first! If you can imagine an accident arising out of a situation, don't get into that situation.

Which are **BOLDFACE, NO-EXCEPTION** rules?
- Safety rules are for everyone, not just students or beginners, but instructors as well.
- Students will be supervised at all times.
- Horse areas are hard-hat areas. This means you must wear and fasten your approved safety helmet.

Safety rules should cover all aspects of life at the barn, wherever horses and people come into contact with each other. This includes places to ride, proper riding clothes and equipment, and avoiding unsafe situations. Examples of these will be given under the individual sections that follow.

2. Riders
Riding rules (followed by examples)
a. Arena rules
- Students will lead horses to and from the arena and will always close the gate when riding.
- You should, at least, be able to see the feet of the horse in front of you between your horse's ears. If you need to pass, don't. Do a circle if no one is behind you or cut across the arena and find an open spot. Be sure to get permission first.

b. Trail ride rules
- There should be a safety lecture/lesson in which riders must demonstrate their ability to start, stop, and steer.
- Stay in single file and be able to see the feet of the horse in front of you between your horse's ears.
- Keep your back vertical to the horizon going up and down hills. This will feel like leaning back or forward slightly.

c. Pony ride rules
- Pony rides will be walk only.
- All ponies will be saddled and bridled. Remember, your insurance probably doesn't cover pony rides unless you specifically request it.
- All pony riders will wear properly fitted, approved helmets.

3. Requirements for riding
- Trail riders must be at least 12 years old before they can ride without previous experience.
- Students should be at least 10 years of age. If you have ponies that will longe safely, you may wish to accept younger students.

Clothing
- All riders must wear boots with at least a one-half-inch heel. These protect the

feet more than tennis shoes will and keep feet from slipping through the stirrups. Boots or shoes specifically designed for riding will be worn while working around horses as well as while mounted.

- ASTM/SEI–approved helmets will be worn by all riders and instructors, not just children, while working around horses and while mounted.
- Long pants will be worn by all riders when mounted. No sweats are permitted, because they tend to ride up the leg and do not provide adequate protection.

Evaluation of riders
- All riders are evaluated according to previous riding experience and size, and then matched with an appropriate horse.
- A rider shall be denied the privilege of riding if she does not abide by the safety rules.

Do not assume that riders are as good or as poor as they say. It may be necessary to switch to a different horse after just one ride or even during the first ride. It's also important for a rider, especially a beginner, to be compatible with a horse's personality. Putting a quiet, shy person with a more assertive horse is not a good idea.

Supervision of riders
- Never leave students unattended in the barn.
- They also shall not go into any stalls with a horse unless supervised.
- Watch students as they clean hooves; they tend to put their own feet down where the horse will put his.

4. Horses
a. Know your horses
- How many school horses do you have? What are their levels?
- How many horses longe safely?
- Have they been trained English? Western? to drive?

Instructors must know the temperament and abilities of each horse before the student gets on. This means working around and getting on each horse themselves. They should not rely on someone else to tell them about a horse. Instructors must also be able properly to school horses to the level at which they are instructing.

b. Ground handling
Tying (followed by examples)
- Always use a quick-release knot when tying. There are many ways to tie a quick-release knot. Some are better than others, but all are better than using a regular knot. The purpose in using a quick-release knot is to free the horse as quickly as possible in an emergency or to avoid an accident.
- Tie only to sturdy posts or rails that will not come out if the horse pulls back.
- Never tie a horse with the reins.
- Tie horses eye high and at an arm's length. Their eye, not yours.

Working around horses

- Stay as close to the shoulder as possible. The shoulder is a neutral zone in which the horse feels least threatened.
- Touch and speak softly to the horse at all times. Horses are sensitive and will respond negatively to loud or aggressive handling.
- When working with the feet or legs, never kneel or sit on the ground. If the horse startles, you need to be able to spring quickly out of the way.

To the horse, we smell like a predator because we are meat eaters. You must remember that each horse you work with needs to be able to trust you. If you act like a predator, being loud or abusive, there will be no trust.

The horse's well-being

- If a horse is injured or unsound, it must not be ridden.
- If the weather is blustery, changeable, recently cool, or if the horse wasn't turned out or ridden the day before, longe him or ride him first yourself.
- Be sure all tack fits properly and is correctly adjusted.

Remember, if your horse feels good and is happy, you will receive a quicker and better response throughout your ride, provided your cues or aids are correct. When a horse is labeled "crabby" or "sour," many times it is due to an ill-fitting piece of tack or an unnoticed lameness or injury. This is the instructor's fault, and the horse must not be punished.

5. General information

a. **Policies and procedures:** When you write your policies and your procedures, be sure that they are written clearly and that thorough explanations are given. Emphasize to your staff the importance of knowing these policies and procedures and make sure they are adhered to by everyone.

Procedures should be designed to best fulfill the needs of your barn. All rules and procedures should be thoroughly explained and adhered to at all times.

b. **Expectations of staff:** Expectations should be carefully thought out and explained during the initial interview, not after the person is hired. You may want to have a prospective employee read your staff manual before you hire her. This will give her an idea of what to expect. Ask her if she has any questions and whether she understands the policies and procedures. You should not assume someone understood everything. Examples:

- Professionalism is expected at all times.
- Dress neatly and appropriately for the style of riding you are teaching.
- Relationships other than instructor-student are strictly prohibited. Any infractions of this rule will be grounds for dismissal.

c. **Lessons should be safe and creative:** They must be planned and have a goal. Do not ask a student to perform a task on a horse that you, yourself, are not able to perform or have not performed on that horse. Example:

- Always have with you in the lesson your Lexington-approved helmet, a knife, and, if you take the students away from the barn, a first-aid kit.

d. Dealing with customers: Proper communication skills are essential when dealing with customers and prospective customers. You must be sure your staff knows how to speak clearly and be courteous. They need not be afraid to approach someone and speak with confidence. It must also be clear that if a staff member is in a bad mood, or involved in a conflict with someone else, the conflict should be set aside and not be made apparent to the customer. Examples:

- If someone you don't know comes into the barn, do not ignore him. Acknowledge him in a friendly, professional way by saying, "Hi, may I help you?" or "Are you looking for the manager?"
- When taking phone messages, always write down the caller's name, message, and phone number, then repeat it back to him and ask him to spell his name.

e. Dealing with other staff: Have a definite chain of command so that all will know who they are responsible to, for example:

STABLE OWNER

Office staff   Barn Manager   Trainer

Assistant Manager   Instructors

Grooms and Stable Help

Assistant or Junior Instructors

Your chain of command may be different, but it should be stated clearly.

A private relationship between staff members is discouraged unless the staff members are mature enough to keep it away from the barn.

Communication is important within the staff itself. Horse and riding terms and directions on how to do things must be the same within the staff to avoid misunderstanding. For instance, longeing may mean running the horse around a round pen with a halter on, or it may mean tacking up the horse with saddle, bridle, and side reins and schooling him in the round pen. These things must be made clear or else an instruction like "Longe Ol' Dobbin" is ambiguous and may not result in the intended activity.

Resolution of conflict is essential within the staff. This means that if there is disagreement among staff members (or with anyone else, for that matter) they must learn to resolve it calmly and maturely among themselves. If this cannot be accomplished, a supervisor (someone higher in the chain of command who is able to give neutral opinions) should be consulted. Do not involve students, customers, or other people who have no business being involved.

B. Key Points in Teaching

1. Dealing with students
a. Physical capabilities (followed by examples)

- Consider that many young or inexperienced riders don't have the muscle development to handle the effort it takes to ride. If they are pushed beyond their capabilities, they will be more likely to sustain painful injury.

b. **Mental capabilities**
- When learning to ride, it takes a lot of concentration to think about how everything that an instructor says is going to fit together. This may cause stress.
- Students must be brought along slowly, correctly, and with exercises so that they are able to stay relaxed and have a positive experience.

c. **Attitude:** Being creative and/or varying the location of the lessons (outdoors, indoors, trail rides) can be an effective way to maintain a positive frame of mind and will aid in the progress of the student. The best time for learning is when both horse and rider are relaxed. Maintaining a relaxed and positive attitude is essential for both rider and instructor. The horse can feel when a rider is tense, stiff, or nervous and will respond by tensing his own muscles. Then all freedom of movement is lost. Also, a rider can sense when the instructor is upset or in a bad mood. This may cause the rider to become uneasy, tense, or fearful and, again, relaxation is lost.

2. Dealing with horses

Think before you act! An instructor must think carefully about what the horse is to do and then think about what she needs to do to make him do it. If she thinks first, she won't confuse the horse with the wrong cue or aid and get a wrong, or confused, response. An instructor also must think carefully when things aren't going well. Before the instructor uses force or punishes the horse, she must be sure that she is not the one who has made the mistake and left out a step or used an incorrect cue or aid.

3. Additional material

- Use excerpts from your favorite riding/instructing books.
- Use "handouts" on teaching techniques, strategy situations, and so on.

C. Risk Management

Risk management is what you do in order to prevent accidents. Do this by educating your staff, maintaining facilities and horses, and checking tack and equipment for repair or replacement. If you can foresee an accident happening in a certain situation, you must prevent the situation.

D. Emergency Procedures for People

What to do when a rider falls (followed by examples)
- Immediately stop all other riders.
- Ask if the person is all right.
- Always fill out an accident report.
- Interview witnesses while the incident is fresh, not overblown.

Calling 911
- Stay calm.
- Tell the person who answers everything you know about the condition of the rider.
- Stay on the line until the person hangs up.
- Make sure medical release volume goes with the injured person.

Procedures vary depending on where you are located. Call your local American Red Cross or Emergency Medical Service for the best advice on this procedure. The general guideline is to have as many facts as you can about the accident, the vital signs of the injured person, and to stay on the line until you are disconnected.

Filling out accident reports:

There are many different kinds of forms. Your own form might include:
- Name of the injured person
- Name of the horse
- What happened
- Where it happened
- Names of witnesses — and statements
- What was done for the injured person

The most important thing about filling out an accident report is to state the facts only. Do not write an endless monologue about the whole ordeal. This is an example of an accident report that is poor because it contains unnecessary detail:

"John and Dusty began trotting, and everything started out fine. Then Johnny started gripping with his legs, which he usually doesn't do, and Dusty started to trot faster. They came up behind Sugar, who is a slow trotter, and Dusty and Sugar hate each other. Johnny was getting really scared and tense and started yelling when he couldn't steer Dusty far enough away from Sugar as they were passing. Sugar kicked Dusty because she hates him and when Dusty shied away quickly, Johnny fell off. He sat there for a few minutes but wasn't hurt."

This is better:

"Group was trotting. Dusty passed Sugar. Sugar kicked Dusty. Dusty shied, and Johnny fell off. Johnny was scared but unhurt."

Medical Consent to Treatment Forms

Keep all the forms in a single binder located at _____. The binder must go to the hospital with every minor. The forms should be filled out by everyone who rides your horses. The form should give permission for you to take someone to the hospital in case of an accident and to be treated by the hospital staff. This form should include:

- Name, address, and phone number
- Parents' names (if rider is a minor)
- Insurance company and policy number
- Signature of parent (if student is a minor)

(See Appendix A for more about medical consent to treatment forms.)

Emergency Equipment

- *Walkie-talkies:* These can be used on trail rides in order for the guides to communicate more effectively. We also recommend that there be a receiver at the barn so that, in case of emergency, extra help can be contacted on the spot. Walkie-talkies are also helpful when one instructor is in the arena and another is in the barn.
- *Whistles:* Loud referee whistles are best utilized as an emergency signal. They will cut through a lot of extra noise and are great for use between the barn and arena. Trail rides may go too far away for them to be effective.
- *Bullhorn:* This is another tool to be used primarily in the arena. It can be used to call someone at the barn or in instructing a larger group in a large arena.

Emergency Procedures for Horses

State in your manual the normal horse vital signs and be sure each member of the staff knows how to take them.

Normal Vital Signs
- Temperature (99–101°F)
- Pulse (32–44 beats per minute; higher in foals)
- Respiration (8–16 breaths per minute)
- Capillary refill (pinch test on gums, 2 seconds)
- Test for dehydration (pinch test on neck, 1–2 seconds)

Develop a procedure for evaluating the problem.
When a Horse is Lame
- Which leg is it?
- Is it swollen?
- Is it hot?

When a Horse has a Major Laceration
- Where is it located?
- How deep is it?
- Is it still bleeding?

If Internal Problems are Suspected
- Has he eaten his feed or had water?
- Check hydration and capillary refill.
- Any signs of discomfort?
- Check temperature, pulse, and respiration.

Calling the veterinarian. Many veterinarians will ask for the horse's vital signs (temperature, pulse, respiration, and capillary refill) on the phone. Be prepared to give them to him. Contact your veterinarian in advance to ask what he specifically would like you to do. Write it down and inform all staff. If something is wrong with a horse and you're not sure whether to call the veterinarian, call him anyway. It doesn't cost anything to ask a few questions.

Definitions, symptoms, and treatment of common problems including:
- Bleeding and puncture wounds
- Lameness (founder, abscess)
- Internal sickness (colic, choke)

Again, contact your veterinarian about treatment procedures to include in your manual. He may also give more detailed definitions of problems and their symptoms than you can get from a book.

First-Aid Kits

For the best advice on compiling first-aid kits for people and horses, contact your physician and veterinarian. They will, most likely, be attending to the injured person or horse, so you should follow their guidelines. Never second-guess them.

We require all staff to be certified in standard first aid. This will help minimize insurance rates and ensure that all have been informed and taught how to handle an accident.
- Kit for people: antibiotic ointment, adhesive bandages, triangle bandage, gauze pads
- Kit for horses: Betadine solution, topical antibiotic cream, nonstick gauze pads, vet wrap

In Case of Fire

In the Barn
- Be sure fire extinguishers are checked every six months and replaced when needed. They should also be replaced if they've been used. All important phone numbers must be posted by each phone.
- Stay calm.
- Get people out first.
- Call the fire department.
- Get horses out second if it's not too dangerous (ask your veterinarian how to get horses out safely).

On Trail Rides
- If there is a forest fire or grass fire, you must always have a way out or an alternative route.
- Trail guides must be familiar with the whole area and how it relates to the barn in case cross-country riding is needed to escape a fire.

E. Barn Rules

When creating barn rules, you not only have to set and enforce each rule, but you also must be able to explain the reasons why each rule is needed.

Your list of rules must be posted and will cover conduct, attire, equipment use, horse sense, and restricted areas.

Conduct

Smoking is not allowed in or within 50 feet of the barn. Why? Smoking is a fire hazard. We don't want to burn a barn down because of a cigarette that didn't quite get put out.

Please don't run in the barn area or around the horses. Why? Running invites tripping, slipping, and falling, any of which can cause an accident. Running also spooks horses in or out of the barn.

Attire

ASTM/SEI–approved riding helmets are required at all times when working around and riding horses. Why? Horses are dangerous and can cause situations that put people at risk. Don't lose your head!

Boots with at least a one-half-inch heel will be worn at all times while working around and riding horses. Why? Boots are sturdier and will protect your feet better than can tennis shoes or sandals. The one-half-inch heel will help keep your foot from sliding through the stirrups.

Equipment Use

If you use a piece of equipment, put it back where it belongs. Why? This keeps everything neat, organized, and easier to find. It is very irritating to have to hunt for the apple picker every time you need it.

Do not let tack drag on the ground. Why? It makes the leather extremely dirty, and you will have to clean it more often. There's also a good chance you or the horse will step on it, break it, or tear it.

Horse Sense

Never hand-feed the horses. Why? Horses may mistake fingers for carrots and, if hand-fed often, can become nippy. Put treats in a bucket or feed box.

Always use a quick-release knot when tying horses. Why? If there's an emergency and your horse needs to get away now, it's the fastest knot to untie.

Restricted areas

Please respect restriction signs on pastures and paddocks. Why? Some places are for authorized staff only because of the likelihood that loose horses will be there.

Do not climb in the hayloft. Why? There are a lot of holes between the bales and if they become loose toward the edge, you could slip and fall out of the loft. Also, you could encounter snakes that may live among the bales.

F. Equipment Care

Leather tack. To clean: Use a soft to medium sponge or cloth in a circular motion to rub in the cleaner and/or conditioner. You don't want to scratch the leather with hard brushes. Use glycerin soap to clean the leather, and then leather conditioner to finish. Bridles used frequently (three to four times a week) should be cleaned at least every two to three weeks. Rinse bits after each use.

To inspect: Check tack for cracks or broken parts before each use. Damaged leather should be repaired or replaced before it is used. Be sure to check hardware, too.

Nonleather tack. To clean: Blankets should be hand-washed and hung to dry. Scrub halters with a mild soap and rinse thoroughly. Halters should be cleaned when greasy dirt and hair starts to accumulate on the underside.

To inspect: Nonleather tack must also be checked frequently for repair or replacement. (Lead ropes should be included.) Check snaps sturdiness and see that rope is not frayed.

Grooming tools. If possible, each horse should have his own set of brushes. Actual washing of brushes is required less frequently if brushes are cleaned after each use.

If you use clippers, oil them before and after each use. Apply blade wash frequently during the clipping.

Storage of tack. All tack should be stored in a clean, dry, rodent-free room. Do not store tack in feed or tool rooms. Keep feed and tack rooms neat and well organized.

G. Horse Care

Grooming. What tools do you use? You'll need a curry comb, dandy brush, body brush, and hoof pick. How often do you use them? Thoroughly groom the horse before and after each riding. Grooming is also a time to check the horse for soreness or injury, so take your time.

Regular maintenance. Horses are healthier and happier if they are groomed on a regular schedule.

Daily work schedule. Trail horses should not work more than eight hours a day, and no more than four hours without a break.

Deworming. Deworm horses every six to eight weeks. Rotate dewormer and use an ivermectin brand in the spring and fall.

Trimming and shoeing. Horses' feet should be trimmed or shod every six to eight weeks.

Teeth floating Horses should have their teeth floated at least once a year after the age of 4.

Reschooling school horses. School horses tend to get "sour" if you use them over and over for the same thing, especially horses for beginners. Rotate them, if possible, to give them time off or time to be reschooled and/or reevaluated for their level of performance.

H. Feeding

All horses have different nutritional requirements. What they are fed depends upon their age and type of work. It is best to feed horses on a regular schedule. Your veterinarian can give you the best advice on what kinds of feed, and their nutritional value, are available in your area.

Grain. Oats, corn, milo, and barley are high in carbohydrates, which provide energy. Protein is also provided. Grains, except corn, lack minerals and have almost no vitamin A.

Grain mixes. "Sweet feed" is a mixture of oats, corn, and barley. The grains are usually cracked or rolled and then coated with molasses.

Roughage. Hay and pasture grass are high in fiber and contribute energy, protein, and minerals. The different types of hay also vary in nutritional value. For instance, alfalfa hay is much higher in protein than is bromegrass. It is also harder to digest, though, and should be fed more conservatively.

Vitamins and supplements. Vitamins help the body utilize nutrients for growth, maintenance, and reproduction. Add supplements to feed if a horse's diet is deficient in a certain area. Supplements are available in protein, mineral, and energy forms, or in combinations of these. Fresh, clean water and salt blocks must always be available to the horse. Water helps deliver nutrients throughout the body, aids in digestion, and helps regulate body temperature.

I. Common Problems and Situations

List possible problems or situations so your staff will become aware of how to handle them.

Problems in teaching

Problem: Parents stand by the arena and talk to the student throughout the lesson.

Solution: Make it a policy that although all parents may watch, they are not to talk because it interrupts the student's concentration and ability to listen to the instructor. You might put chairs behind a fence or out of the way to make it clear that they are not to participate in the lesson.

Problems in stable management

Problem: Staff may get lazy about paperwork, such as record keeping or taking messages.

Solution: Be sure records are organized in a book or folder that is easily accessible for regular updates. Keep a pen and paper by each phone.

Problems in horse handling

Problem: Sometimes people will get too relaxed around horses and disregard safety rules. For instance, leading the horse by the end of the lead rope and walking five feet in front of him creates the potential for a dangerous situation.

Solution: Adopt a "gotcha" policy. Whoever catches someone being unsafe is to inform the manager or owner, and the unsafe person has to do an hour's work for the person who caught him. With kids or customers, the "penalty" might be saddling, horse bathing, or mane pulling, for example.

Problems in riding

Problem: Many green students will constantly nag at a horse or let him get away with not doing what he is supposed to do.

Solution: Evaluate school horses frequently by getting on yourself and schooling them back to the level at which they should be performing, or vary their work schedule to include some relaxing or fun exercises, such as trail rides or cross-country gallops.

Rainy-day activities and ground schools. These should be games, projects, talks, or quizzes that students can do when they are not able to ride.

J. Games

1. "Bit game." Kids pair up — one is the rider and the other is the horse. The rider puts a long strand (three feet) of clean string or twine in the "horse's" mouth and holds the ends like reins, standing behind the "horse." Riders are asked to walk, turn, stop, and back their "horses." This is fun, and students learn about responsiveness. It also gives them a chance to feel what the horse feels.

2. "Tape the part on the horse." After students have learned the parts of the horse, they split into teams and alternate taping paper parts on a horse. Be sure the horse you choose stands well and can tolerate having pieces of paper taped all over his body. The team with the most correctly placed parts wins.

K. Horse-Sense Talks

1. Evolution of the horse
2. Nutrition and feeding of the horse
3. Parts of . . . classes: can include horse, saddles, bridles. When the lesson is on bridle parts, it is also fun to have the instructor take the bridle completely apart and ask a student to put it back together.

Camp considerations. You may want to include an outline of your daily/weekly schedule. Summer staff needs to be able to organize and produce the program within a short (two to three weeks, sometimes less) period of time. They need to know the goals of the program.

If a barn staff member feels a rider is not capable of handling a particular horse, he has the authority to deny that rider's choice or to switch the rider to another horse.

Barn staff has authority over counselors and other camp staff when they are in the barn.

You may think of other topics to include in your manual, depending upon your barn and staff priorities. Remember, everything your staff is responsible for must be covered in the manual. It is your proof that you have procedures in place and that your staff has been informed of them.

Appendix C

ABOUT THE AAHS

The American Association for Horsemanship Safety Inc. (AAHS) is a tax-exempt, 501(c)(3) nonprofit, educational corporation founded in July 1995 with an eye toward insulating riding instructors and site occupiers from liability suits.

The AAHS is dedicated to promoting safety on and around horses. AAHS-certified instructors first and foremost are equestrian lifeguards. Their training focuses on providing a safe environment in which to ride. The safe-riding environment includes activities involving the horse during routine training, boarding, showing, lessons, and camp/guest ranch activities.

AAHS does not favor one riding style over another. The association is concerned with correct balance on any type of horse and with an AAHS-certified instructor's ability to assist students in finding their balance as safely and quickly as possible.

AAHS and Negligence Laws

The AAHS program has its basis in current liability law and a desire to help prevent accidents due to ignorance and incompetence. The association's goal is to show instructors how to be less vulnerable to lawsuits on most issues. Two AAHS officers are attorneys.

AAHS Web Site

The AAHS Web Site is the largest compilation of current horse-related legislation and litigation. It keeps members up to date on current litigation and articles on horse-related negligence law. It also contains horse-related news articles that have appeared in English-language newspapers, horse laughs, and safety information. The address is **http://www.law.utexas.edu/dawson/**

AAHS Certification

Anyone interested in AAHS certification may contact the AAHS office and request information on the types of certification available. We have certification programs for nonriding supervisors of schools, barns, and horse shows as well as assistant riding instructors. We offer certification in Instructor Basics and for Head Instructors.

The certification program is offered at two locations year-round on an individual basis. It is possible for AAHS to arrange for a clinician to come to a site in your area. Clinics are limited to 10 active participants when only one clinician is present. It is the responsibility of the host site to advertise and make arrangements for the clinic. AAHS clinicians charge a flat rate per day, plus expenses.

Seminars and workshops on safety and dealing wth negligence law as it affects riding instructors and stables also are available through the AAHS.

American Association for Horsemanship Safety
Drawer 39
Fentress, TX 78622
(512) 488-2128 (office)
(512) 488-2220 (house and barn)

Articles on safe horsemanship, horses in the news, and information about legal liability statutes and case law can be explored on our Web Site: http://www.law.utexas.edu/dawson

AAHS Certification Clinic — 40 Hours

Sample Schedule of Lectures and Activities in 4-day Format
The order may vary.

Day One
Registration: get acquainted; safety tour
Introduction: history of AAHS; clinic goals
Risk Management Lecture: how to make yourself more resistant to litigation
Horse Science: lecture one — horse psychology and physiology
Preparing to Ride Safely: equipment, grooming, tacking up, mounting, dismounting
Candidate Mounted Evaluation: mount and ride in own style, demonstrate pattern
The Lesson: warm-up, skill practice, game, review
Evaluation of Mounted Session
Training techniques, school horse problems, or veterinarian and/or farrier demonstration
Exam

Day Two
Legislation and Standards
Liability: case histories
Stable Management: organization, design, traffic, records
Trail Ride/Lesson Procedure: safety checks, preride demonstration
Lineup, mounting, warm-up, traffic rules
Brief trail ride or sample drill team and mounted games
Strategy quiz; emergency procedures

Effective Communication: teaching by exercises, games
Teaching assignments; lesson plans

Day Three
Horse Science Lecture Two and Mounted Sessions
Critique
Teaching Techniques
Horse Science Lecture Three and Mounted Sessions

Day Four
Mounted Sessions
Written Examination
Instructional Practical Examination
Individual Conferences
Lunch may be made available on the grounds or be free time away from the facility.

Appendix D

RECOMMENDED READING

Foreman, Monte and Patrick Wyse. *Monte Foreman's Horse-Training Science*. Norman, OK: University of Oklahoma Press, 1983.

Griffin, James M., M.D., and Tom Gore, D.V.M. *Horse Owner's Veterinary Handbook*. New York: Howell Book House, 1989.

Haas, Jesse. *Safe Horse, Safe Rider*. Pownal, VT: Storey Publishing, 1994.

Henriques, Pegotty. *Balanced Riding*. Gaithersburg, MD: Half-Halt Press, 1987.

Hill, Cherry. *Becoming an Effective Rider*. Pownal, VT: Storey Publishing, 1991.

Hill, Cherry. *Making Not Breaking: The First Year Under Saddle*. Ossining, NY: Breakthrough Publications, 1992.

Hill, Cherry. *101 Arena Exercises*. Pownal, VT: Storey Publishing, 1995.

Hunt, Ray. *Think Harmony with Horses*. Fresno, CA: Pioneer Publishing Co., 1991.

Loving, Nancy, D.V.M. *Veterinary Manual for the Performance Horse*. Grand Prairie, TX: Equine Research Inc., 1993.

Lyons, John, with Sinclair Browning. *Lyons on Horses*. New York: Doubleday, 1991.

McBane, Susan. *Poor Richard's Horse Keeper*. Ossining, NY: Breakthrough Publications, 1993.

Museler, Wilhelm. *Riding Logic*. Edited by K.A. von Ziegner. Arco Publishing, 1983.

Pinch, Dorothy Henderson. *Happy Horsemanship*. New York: Simon & Schuster, 1992.

Strickland, Charlene. *Western Riding*. Pownal, VT: Storey Publications, 1995.

Swift, Sally. *Centered Riding*. New York: St. Martins/Malek, 1985.

von Ziegner, K.A. *The Basics*. Xenophon Press, 1995.

INDEX

OTHER STOREY TITLES YOU WILL ENJOY

Becoming an Effective Rider: Developing Your Mind and Body for Balance and Unity, by Cherry Hill. Teaches riders how to evaluate their own skills, plan a work session, get maximum use out of lesson time, set goals and achieve them, and protect themselves from injury. 192 pages. Paperback. ISBN #0-88266-688-6.

From the Center of the Ring: An Inside View of Horse Competitions, by Cherry Hill. Covers all aspects of equestrian competition, both English and Western. 192 pages. Paperback. ISBN #0-88266-494-8.

Horse Handling & Grooming: A Step-by-Step Photographic Guide, by Cherry Hill. For both beginners and experienced riders, this user-friendly guide to essential skills includes feeding, haltering, tying, grooming, clipping, bathing, braiding, and blanketing. 144 pages. Paperback. ISBN #0-88266-956-7.

Horse Health Care: A Step-by-Step Photographic Guide, by Cherry Hill. Explains bandaging, giving shots, examining teeth, deworming, and preventive care. Exercising and cooling down, hoof care, and tending wounds are depicted, along with taking a horse's temperature, and determining pulse and respiration rates. 160 pages. Paperback. ISBN #0-88266-955-9.

Horsekeeping on a Small Acreage: Facilities Design and Management, by Cherry Hill. Horse trainer, Cherry Hill, describes the essentials for designing safe and functional facilities. 192 pages. Paperback. ISBN #0-88266-596-0.

Horse Sense: A Complete Guide to Horse Selection & Care, by John J. Mettler, Jr., D.V.M. The basics on selecting, housing, fencing, and feeding a horse including information on immunizations, dental care, and breeding. 160 pages. Paperback. ISBN #0-88266-545-6.

101 Arena Exercises: A Ringside Guide for Horse & Rider, by Cherry Hill. A ringside exercise book for riders who want to improve their own and their horse's skills. Classic exercises and original patterns and drills presented in a unique "read and ride" format. 224 pages. Paperback. ISBN #0-88266-316-X.

Safe Horse, Safe Rider: A Young Rider's Guide to Responsible Horsekeeping, by Jessie Haas. Beginning with understanding the horse and ending with competitions, every chapter includes encouraging ideas for a good relationship. Chapters on horse body language, safe pastures and stables, catching, leading and tying, grooming safety, and riding out. 160 pages. Paperback. ISBN #0-88266-700-9.

Starting & Running Your Own Horse Business, by Mary Ashby McDonald. This essential guide shows readers how to run a successful business — and how to make the most of their investments in horses, facilities, equipment, and time over short- and long-term periods. From general business tips to saving cash on stable management, this book quickly pays for itself. 160 pages. Paperback. ISBN #0-88266-960-5.

Western Riding, by Charlene Strickland. This book goes beyond the traditional teachings to be the rider's one-stop Western riding guide. From a review of breeds and basic handling to enthusiastic instructions on various Western riding disciplines to tips from professional coaches, this book is much more than how to ride, rope, and race. 240 pages. Hardcover. ISBN #0-88266-890-0.

Your Horse: A Step-by-Step Guide to Horse Ownership, by Judy Chapple. Highly readable for all ages and packed with practical information on buying, housing, feeding, training, riding, and handling medical problems. 144 pages. Paperback. ISBN #0-88266-353-4.

Your Pony, Your Horse: A Kid's Guide to Care and Enjoyment, by Cherry Hill. Part of our friendly and encouraging children's animal reference series, featuring information on selection, housing, feeding, health, behavior, and showing in a mature yet easy-to-understand language. 160 pages. Paperback. ISBN #0-88266-908-7.

These books and other Storey books are available at your bookstore, farm store, garden center, or directly from Storey Publishing, Schoolhouse Road, Pownal, Vermont 05261, or by calling 1-800-441-5700. www.storey.com